YOU, ME & WE

DR. ANTHONY HUGHES, PHD, CST

Marriage and Family Therapist and Certified Sex Therapist

YOU, ME & WE

A PRACTICAL GUIDE TO MARITAL INTIMACY

CFI
An imprint of Cedar Fort, Inc.
Springville, Utah

ISBN 13: 978-1-4621-2096-3

Published by CFI, an imprint of Cedar Fort, Inc.
2373 W. 700 S., Springville, UT 84663
Distributed by Cedar Fort, Inc., www.cedarfort.com

LIBRARY OF CONGRESS CATALOGING-IN-PUBLICATION DATA

Names: Hughes, Anthony A. (Anthony Allen), 1982- author.
Title: You, me, and we : a practical guide to marital intimacy / Dr. Anthony
   A. Hughes, PhD.
Description: Springville, Utah : CFI, An imprint of Cedar Fort, Inc., [2017]
   | Includes bibliographical references and index.
Identifiers: LCCN 2017038595 (print) | LCCN 2017042589 (ebook) | ISBN
   9781462128358 (epub and Moby) | ISBN 9781462120963 ([perfect] : alk. paper)
Subjects: LCSH: Sex in marriage--Religious aspects--Church of Jesus Christ of
   Latter-day Saints. | Sex in marriage--Religious aspects--Mormon Church. |
   Intimacy (Psychology)--Religious aspects--Church of Jesus Christ of
   Latter-day Saints. | Intimacy (Psychology)--Religious aspects--Mormon
   Church.
Classification: LCC BX8643.S49 (ebook) | LCC BX8643.S49 H84 2017 (print) |
   DDC 248.8/44--dc23
LC record available at https://lccn.loc.gov/2017038595

Cover design by Jeff Harvey
Cover design © 2017 by Cedar Fort, Inc.
Edited by Deborah Spencer and Emily Chambers
Typeset by Kaitlin Barwick

Printed in the United States of America

10 9 8 7 6 5 4 3 2 1

Printed on acid-free paper

DEDICATION

I count myself fortunate to be writing this dedication. I know how rare it is to publish a book with a reputable publisher. It is not without merit that I find myself in this situation. However, this merit achieved is only through the grace and love of God. He has been and is without question the perfect parent. All that I do and all that I am is first and foremost because of Him. It is my prayer that at the end of my life I can look back and say firmly that my life was a living dedication to Him.

Because of God's grace and love I can write the rest of this dedication. My wife, Hayley, has created the home I needed to flourish and become as an adult. After God and with the needed base that my parents created and maintain, she is responsible for all that I have achieved. I not only dedicate this book to her, but affirm she is my coauthor in life and deed.

Liam, Nolan, Isabelle, and our baby still with mom, you are my drive, my reason, the breath to my life. While you rest soundly like angles cozy in your beds, your existence fills my soul with fire and I write. Your pictures, your messages, your voices sound the call that musters the imagination from within and I create. I dedicate my unyielding endurance and creation to you.

Mom and dad you have spoken to a part deep within me that is only identifiable as my spirit. While you clothed me, fed me, taught me, kept me safe, somehow you reached my spirit and beckoned its presence. I feel as though it is going to burst from my body and glisten in the light. It transcends all Earthly challenge and fear and rings loudly and guides gently but majestically. All that is within is dedicated to you both.

ALSO BY

DR. ANTHONY HUGHES

What Your Parents Didn't Tell You about Sex:
An LDS Guide to Sexual Intimacy

CONTENTS

CONTENTS

PREFACE

I am asked by most of my clients and those who know what I do for my career, "Why did you decide to go into sex therapy?" I feel it is important to answer this question so that you gain some insight into my interest in this field and into who I am. I grew up in Springville, Utah, where I was raised in a predominantly Latter-day Saint (LDS) community. I picked up pretty quickly that sexuality was not something that was freely discussed. Being a lifelong student of the human experience, I could see that this would most likely lead to issues in couples' sexual relationships and their relationships as a whole. As I began studying the human experience on a scholastic level at Brigham Young University, I could see that the limited communication surrounding sexuality, as well as the general lack of sexual experience among fellow members of my faith, could and would very well lead to issues in sexual intimacy—not to mention that the cards were already stacked against couples, as sex is one of the top reasons that couples get divorced both in conservative groups and in nonreligious or liberal populations. Upon beginning my clinical graduate work at Brigham Young University, I began to amass mounting evidence that what I had hypothesized, read, learned, and heard from others was true. There is a large need among fellow members of my faith to address issues of sexuality. My ease in discussing sexual matters with my clients produced an ideal climate to discuss sexual dysfunctions and dissatisfactions. These experiences were the seeds of my career in sex therapy. I have been ever grateful for the rewarding work I do on a daily basis.

I want to start out this book by stating that the assignments, or as I call them activities, herein will need to be filtered through your own personal views, beliefs, and standards. The longer I do work in this field, the more I see differences in the beliefs of members of our common faith. I by no means want you to think that you must do what is provided in this book, unless you feel your own desire to do so. I would never want to be the reason that anyone gets in trouble with their God. I have only included those assignments that actual members of our faith have felt confident in performing. All others—and believe me, there are a lot of additional assignments in the sex therapy literature that have not been selected by members of our faith—have been left out.

This manuscript is not an official publication of The Church of Jesus Christ of Latter-day Saints. The views and insights given herein are of the author, those referenced, academic, or general knowledge and do not reflect those opinions of the Church.

INTRODUCTION

*A*s a therapist specializing in sex therapy within a conservative pocket of the world, I have had countless colleagues contact me looking for a book that they can refer to their clients that explicitly details sexual relationships, processes, and important nuances from an LDS gospel–centered approach. Colleagues and clients alike have found that the current literature written by LDS authors, while informative and vital, does not go into the sexual depth and explicit detail that they or their clients need. In part, this is why I have decided to embark on this quest. I have only included aspects of sexuality that I feel have been underrepresented or left out by these other amazing authors. Please visit my website, covenantsextherapy.com, which will direct you to these other well-written books by LDS authors.

This book is meant to be an easy read that will provide the reader with all of the pertinent information that they need for satisfying and fulfilling sexual relationships with their spouses. Because of this, I will be direct and to the point. We are all adults and deserve straightforward talk. I know that, like my own, your lives are full of activities and events that pull you every which way. Therefore, each chapter is filled with several significant concepts, homework assignments (I will call them activities), or teachings for the individual and couple. The works contained in this book are a compilation of the very best research, theories, and therapeutic anecdotes. Please take the time to soak in each paragraph, as I have put in a lot of time making sure each is filled with important information.

There are several examples that I have included in this book to illustrate points or application of principles. None of what I have included will breach confidentiality. The names I use for the couples in therapy have been altered for this book. I have also merged client experiences so that I am not telling the story of any specific individual or couple. I am confident you will find these anecdotes helpful.

I have been asked to include some thoughts for parents trying to raise children who do not encounter their same sexual hardships and single individuals who have asked for a chapter or thoughts applicable to them. I have found that these requests are needed as I have trying to shift the LDS culture to be more sex positive. I have included a few notes throughout the book and a chapter for premarital couples.

Before I jump in, I would like to tell you a few crucial things about me, other than my credentials. I *love* my work. I find *great joy* in my clients. I have an unshakable belief in the importance of helping couples have fulfilling sexual relationships. Let's get started.

"SAAM" SEXUAL ATTENTIVENESS & ACCOUNTABILITY MODEL

I have developed a therapeutic model that works quite well in therapy for our clients. It is called Sexual Attentiveness and Accountability Model or "SAAM." I would like to share SAAM with all of you as you go on your sexual journey and believe that you will find it equally as beneficial as my clients do. Now I do not typically tell my clients that we are following this model, but instead use SAAM as a framework for all that I do as I work to help couples improve their sexual relationships. This book and the principles within will be best used through the lens of SAAM. I will try to save you by leaving the research to a minimum and I will discuss the theory behind this model in an easy-to-understand way. I believe that you will enjoy this unique addition to the field of sex therapy that has been specifically developed for work with members of the LDS faith.

Sex therapy has come a long way since its infancy. Just about any sound theoretical model nowadays incorporates a broader contextual viewpoint rather than the more limited individualistic or narrow view as was the case at the beginning of the field of sex therapy. My model is nested within this cutting-edge viewpoint.

SAAM uses the term "systems" to analyze the intricate and complex nature of this broad, modern view. There are only two types of systems in my model. The first are "systems within." There are factors that impact our sexuality that emerge from all systems of an individual. The systems from within include an individual's spirit, physiology, psychology, and personality/characteristics. These systems are easier for us to conceptualize in isolation of the second set of systems since some of these systems have been the way in which the world has viewed sexuality.

For example, for years now, there have been commercials about medication that can help men with erectile dysfunction. These commercials are pointing to an aspect of the systems within an individual's physiology. They basically say that your body isn't working properly and this medication can help it function as it should. So, what's wrong with this? Nothing, if the real cause of erectile dysfunction is biologically related. There are many physiological causes of sexual dysfunction or complaints. Prostate cancer or enlargement is one such physiological cause of erectile dysfunction. That is to say that there is a problem with a system within the individual. As a side note, the pharmaceutical companies have been trying for years to develop a similar drug for women to engender sexual desire. Interestingly they have been perplexed, as female sexuality is a lot more complex. What I hope to accomplish here is not to provide you with a long list of the physiological causes of sexual dysfunctions or issues, but to open your mind to how the systems within impact our sexuality. I will do the same with the second set: systems without.

Depression and anxiety are but a few psychological diagnoses that are highly correlated with sexual issues. When someone is depressed, they have a difficult time finding joy in things that they used to find joy and fulfillment in. It becomes nearly impossible to think that going on a run will help the depressed spouse feel at peace or happy. Instead they think "It does look nice out. It might be fun to go on my old running trail. I'm just so tired though. Running will probably just make me that much more exhausted. It might frustrate me more with my life since I'm not in the shape I used to be in. Let's face it, running isn't going to help. Nothing will help me feel better." At times, the person has a difficult time thinking logically and often these distorted ways of thinking decrease sexual desire. Such thoughts might include thinking "There is nothing interesting about me or worthwhile. I'm as plain and boring as they come. I haven't done anything significant. How can I believe that my wife would care to hear about my life goals or dreams? She's just talking to me because she has to. It's part of her 'job.' She may just be selfish and wanting sex and doesn't really care about me. I bet she's not even thinking about me when we have sex." This form of isolation and shielding from

4

vulnerability caused by depression makes it difficult for a sexual relationship to develop or be fulfilling. The spouse that doesn't think his partner would be interested in his goals, dreams, or life, for that matter, will have a difficult time wanting to be sexual with his spouse. They will have an increasingly difficult time being sexually and spiritually vulnerable during sex if anything sexual does take place. This may be further evidence, misunderstood evidence, mind you, that they are boring, not wanted, and that there is nothing special about them, which only shields them from vulnerability and connection all the more.

Many diagnosable mental struggles have sexual implications. However, one does not have to have a severe or diagnosed psychological problem to be sexually impacted by psychological issues. Fleeting or inconsistent anxiety symptoms can have disastrous sexual implications, for example. A person that is driven by their perfectionism or productivity—anxiety—might not allow themselves the space for orgasm to occur or desire to grow. This person's thoughts might sound a lot like this: "I wish that he would have waited until I finished the online birthday shopping for our son before he initiated sex. Doesn't he see that I'm busy? How can he stop me in the middle of this to make out? I can't just switch from doing this to having sex." The husband may feel as if there is never a good time to initiate sex as she is always busy doing something and he can't ever catch her when she has down time. The wife in this situation might allow the sexually suppressive circumstance of wanting to finish online birthday shopping, or whatever it may be, derail her otherwise enjoyable night. In this example, the wife is frequently busy and otherwise engaged in thought, problem-solving, or action that precludes her from having the space for sexuality to develop and thrive.

An individual's personality/characteristics can also hinder sexuality. Someone that is termed introverted or extroverted may have a difficult time forming the connection requisite for attachment or vulnerability that often precedes and enhances sexuality. For example, the extrovert may be engaged in relationships and activities that prevent them from being present or in the moment for their partner. The connection that would come from these types of interactions can facilitate the emotional climate that engenders sexuality for many.

Spirit is a highly unique component to this model and is scarcely, if ever, mentioned in other theoretical models. Sexuality for the world is physical. No attention or thought is given to the spirit in terms of sexuality. As we know, much of the world doesn't even think that there is anything more than the body. Even in our LDS culture there is a struggle to see how one's spirit is engaged in sexual activity or benefits spiritually from embracing sexuality. Sometimes a person has strayed and struggles connecting to their own spirit and forgets how to connect their spirit to their spouse's in all avenues and especially during sex. Other times the person may not know how to bring their spirit into the bedroom and instead checks it at the door. Instead they only engage in sex as the world teaches us. I must close this brief discussion of the spirit by saying that there is nothing wrong with enjoying the physical. The issue lies in neglecting to incorporate one's spirit into the sexual at all. Only in this way can we truly be congruent children of God.

The second component of SAAM are the "systems from without." These include an individual's upbringing, life events, work, family, friends, family-of-origin, religion, marriage, etc. The systems from without are a lot larger than the systems within. I have only included some of the more significant systems without. When you think of this second group of systems, think of all those things from outside a person that can impact an individual. These are the systems without.

The context of our upbringing has embedded within it lessons about sexuality, both individual sexuality and sexuality with others. Even attempts to eliminate sexual teaching does, in fact, teach about sex. Watching parents have a passionate kiss on occasion throughout the week provides important learning software for the children present. This software helps to program our sexuality by sending us paramount messages. Messages surrounding parents passionately kissing teaches that both women and men value their sexual selves and enjoy moments to share their sexuality. It also provides messages that there is nothing embarrassing or shaming about embracing sexuality or expressing sexuality.

Traumatic experiences leave emotional damage, body memories, flashbacks, and scars that remind us of the dangers that we experienced and aim to teach us about life. Sometimes emotional abuse can lead someone into a web of confusion because they are left uncertain concerning the safety within their relationship. Our minds are wired to keep us safe and to remember those things that help or hinder this safety. When safety is unclear, the insecure person thinks—or rather feels—with safety at the forefront and not necessarily sexual health. An insecure partner may petition for copious amounts of sex to confirm safety or they may avoid sexual advances or individual sexual feelings at every turn to ensure they are not left vulnerable to pain.

Marriage, too, curbs our sexuality in some fashion. There are marriages that encourage healthy sexual expression in a non-shaming way, even when the other partner does not like expressing their sexuality in the same way as their spouse. Exploring what is satisfying about said sexual expression and desiring to be taken into the world of one's spouse shows that it's acceptable to be sexually vulnerable. It illustrates that differences can bring a couple together and helps a person to feel known, understood, or seen in a very intimate way. These are just a few of myriad ways that the systems without a person can impact sexuality.

Now that you have a sound understanding of the two main components of SAAM, I want to give you a visual depiction that might help you as we move into enhancing and healing your sexuality. SAAM uses two visual depictions. First, imagine that your sexuality is a raft floating along a river. There are a few things that the raft comes equipped with. And there are a few other items that you have deemed important for your sexual journey. Some of these may, in fact, be helpful, and some may be harmful to your sexuality. Your raft, its stock, and those things you choose to bring on the raft are the systems within. They are spirit, physiology, psychology, and personality/characteristics.

Lyla and Brody sat in their third therapy session still frustrated that they were not enjoying sex with one another. The couple was successful, educated, and had a really good relationship. They enjoyed doing things together and working alongside one another, and they were confident in their spouse's commitment to the marriage. Brody enjoyed sex at the beginning of their relationship, but this soon took a steep decline as Lyla began expressing her dismay with sexuality. She said that she never enjoyed it and didn't ever have any sexual desire. Brody was a good man and was discontent continuing on in the same way knowing that Lyla was so dissatisfied. After trying to change things on their own, they winded up in my office.

Lyla and Brody were under no illusion that a session or two of therapy would all-of-a-sudden transform their sexual relationship. However, they felt that by now they'd be moving quickly down the path of healing. After three sessions, therapists are usually still trying to gauge the terrain of the individual, couple, and other contextual variables. This third session started to unfold the systems within and their impact on Lyla's sexual landscape. She described her disgust with her vulva. She felt that the hair, lubrication, and the internal nature of her vagina and other sexual/reproductive organs were gross, repulsive, and felt weird to the touch. Lyla didn't like looking at or touching her vulva. She also didn't like that Brody would see and feel it from time to time.

A few sessions later Lyla spoke about her internal dialogue that has been self-deprecating all her life. Lyla had been telling herself that she wasn't special, that she was ugly, that there was nothing unique about her, etc. These self-deprecating thoughts were also present in her appraisal of the sexual aspects of her body, breasts, vulva, vagina, etc. Her confidence was subsequently very low. Lyla's self-confidence and value were impinging upon her sex life. Therapy began to focus on the systems within, namely psychological, that were hijacking her mind and using all of her brainpower toward self-hate. There was no way that this woman who was so repulsed by her vulva, body, and self would want to express herself in a sex-positive way. She just didn't realize that just yet. I realized that the only expression that such a person would want to display would be disgust or sex negative, which was in fact exactly what Lyla and Brody's sex life looked like.

Lyla had a difficult time recognizing that she had so much self-hate because she always felt as though she was just being honest with herself. Therapy addressed truly seeing her self-narrative through writing, which came easy to Lyla. She would also sit up at night staring into the deep darkness of the world through her bedroom window. She felt safe in these places, safe enough to be honest with her spirit. Through identification of her old narrative, Lyla had to face the fact that she had been lying to herself for her entire life. At this point in therapy, the evidence was mounting that contradicted the self-hate that was rampant in her life. Lyla's lie that she was lucky with business and that anyone could find a niche and work their way to success as she did was too elaborate. This was just the tip of the iceberg. She began to find self-worth in who she was and not through external validation, which is what she always had sought. Self-love soon followed. Lyla's narrative that she told herself about her vulva and its role in her life transformed to become more sex positive. She started forming a positive and respectful relationship with her vulva and other sexual organs. Once she could own self-love for the way that she looked, she was able to transform her narrative about her sexuality. Lyla didn't have to look like her sisters to be a bombshell. In this same vein, her vulva didn't have to look any certain way for it to be sexy and attractive. She started loving it just because it was hers and uniquely created. She was only able to go through this sexual narrative transformation because of her self-love that came through addressing her faulty thinking. Lyla and Brody are just one example of how the systems within are at work in sexuality.

The second visual depiction of SAAM is the river. The river is wide at some points and narrow at others. There are sandbars, trees protruding, and fallen timber along the river at certain points. There are smooth and turbulent waters, fast moving and slow waters, high and low tide, storms and clear skies. Broadly, the river represents life. Romantic relationships, experiences, values, work, trauma, family, upbringing, friends, etc. are all factored into the river. The river and all that comes with it are the systems without.

Julie and Scott had been battling what looked to be completely random sexual anxiety that Scott experienced for years in their marriage. Scott said that he enjoyed sex sometimes and then other times his anxiety would take over and he couldn't bring himself to have sex with Julie. He maintained that he thought about being sexual with Julie all the time and that desire wasn't the issue for him. Julie was, by default, the sexual caretaker in their relationship. She would always say that she would be the low desire partner if Scott didn't struggle so much with sexual anxiety.

As the couple got comfortable in therapy, Scott began to mention now and again about the pressures he felt at work, in his calling in the Bishopric, and to be more actively involved with his very busy children. These were typically flippant comments. It became clear to me that the systems without were taking a toll on Scott's sexuality without either partner being aware. His river was frequently surging, sandbars were widespread, and storms were unbridled. Scott's river—his life—was smashing into his raft—sexuality—seemingly unavoidably. At times, he was able to keep his life in check or Julie would unknowingly make a sexual bid when the river was settled, but Scott kept a lot of his distress to himself. He had been taught at a young age that this was just the man's responsibility and that no good would come from him complaining to his wife and stressing her out.

I helped Julie and Scott to see how the systems without were impacting Scott's sexuality. His raft had been battered and stripped of much of its possessions. Scott would have to pull his raft over to the bank and do some repairs and stock up on reserves if he wanted his sexuality to last the course of the river. Scott spoke with the bishop about lightening his load. Scott maintained his role in the Bishopric but shifted some responsibilities to others. This was a new concept for him and required leaning on Julie emotionally to sort out his shame. Scott analyzed his career and realized that he might have to sacrifice a higher sales bracket, which would mean fewer long days and less pay, in order to improve his sexual self. He also spent time working through his shame over not being present for all of his kids' activities. With his extra time away from his other obligations, he was able to go to a few more extracurricular activities, but also spent time caretaking himself by going to the gym. Scott had unrealistic expectations enforced for the role of a father. His dad lost himself in pursuit of always being there for everyone else. Scott unknowingly took upon himself some of his father's characteristics in this regard.

Half a year later, Julie and Scott had the sex life they had been striving for all these years. They couldn't believe it. The couple was overjoyed. Julie was relieved that she no longer had to tote Scott's raft behind hers. In her freedom from hauling Scott's raft, Julie found that she could explore aspects of sexuality that were completely foreign to her. Scott put in a lot of work to let go of the desire to reach expectations he felt from his family-of-origin, work, and the ward. He had to challenge learned perceptions of what a good father, provider, and priesthood holder means. Julie was not absent in these changes. However, in line with SAAM, Scott held himself accountable for making these required changes. This is but one way that the systems without impact sexuality.

Close your eyes for a moment and think of your raft, what comes stock, and what you have brought. Include sex positive and negative. Take note of this in the space below. I hope that it fills more than the space provided.

If you did not write anything down, I want you to ask yourself, "Am I really giving my all to my healing and my relationship?" Now close your eyes again and think of the river and all that it includes. Include sex positive and negative. What is your experience of your river? Please use the space below to answer this pivotal question.

_____

_____

_____

_____

_____

_____

Above, you have defined the systems within your person and the systems without your person. All of these things have an impact on your sexuality. Some of them may have more weight and some may have significantly less. This list is not meant to be fixed, since as the river ebbs and flows, storms and shines, so too does life. Similarly, the raft and its load are anything but permanent as the river acts upon it. It may also change across time. For example, a newborn baby can wreak havoc on one's sexual desire, but the baby only stays newborn for a finite amount of time. Along the river, the items are depleted and wear or are rejuvenated and are improved by the time on the raft or by the river itself. In this way, there is a parallel of the journey of our spirits, physiology, psychology, and personality/characteristics along our life.

Now that you have a general idea of the model, I want to delve into healthy patterns and change. To do this, it is imperative that we explore the two main guideposts of SAAM. The individual has limited control over many aspects of these systems and their impact on sexuality. Cancer, diabetes, sexual abuse, media, culture, male-centric views of sexuality, familial influence, and many more can erode facets of our sexual selves. SAAM posits that we each must be *attentive* to these systemic elements and their impact on sexuality while being individually *accountable* for our own sexual health and well-being. Thus, the name of this theory: Sexual Attentiveness and Accountability Model. The lack of individual attentiveness and accountability undermines the individual's and couple's sexuality. Early awareness, processing, and intervention can speed along sexual healing and get one on the right track for sexual development. However, it is never too late to improve a vital part of one's self—sexuality. Some couples report the most satisfying sexual encounters and experiences in old age. Attentiveness and accountability are the guideposts that SAAM asserts will facilitate healthy development, rectify unhealthy patterns, and enforce positive sexuality.

There are those of you who are reading this book and thinking about your river—life—and are overwhelmed by how frequently it storms on your river or how often you run into sandbars and debris. For example, this may mean having many unhealthy relationships where sexuality was unclean or worldly. These relationships may have led to your current marriage where sexuality is purely physical or solely erotic. Therein your marriage is stunted where it might otherwise become significantly greater or a strength and refuge for you and your spouse. There are others of you that are reading thinking of the tattered nature of the raft—your sexuality—and how ill-equipped your raft was and misguided you were when packing for your sexual journey. This may mean that you have struggled with your thyroids, hormones, negative thought patterns, distraction, and preoccupation throughout your life. This model has been developed for you and every variation between. At times, those with a struggling raft and troublesome river to run may surrender to these systems within and without, but if you have any fight left in you, then out with it and let's chart your course.

Following our guideposts will ensure that we are on the right course. The first guidepost is *attentiveness*. As stated above, you were to write down all of the ways that you have been sexually impacted by systems within and systems without. I desperately hope that you will fill the space, the margin, and write more on separate sheets of paper. Neglecting to do so only illustrates that you are not fully invested in this model since, to truly follow this model, you must be *attentive* to the ways in which you are sexually impacted. As you go through the next few days and weeks, I want you to jot down notes in this book, on your phone, or anywhere, and highlight all those systems that are relevant and how they have transformed your sexual self positively and negatively. If you are reading this book, the chances are there are far more systems that have transformed you in the negative. However, as we move along, we want to rewrite some of these and add more in the sex positive.

If you thought you were done with this guidepost, think again! I now want you to spend some time meditating in the morning or evening with these sexual impacts in mind. Talk to your parents, best friend, spouse, journal, or post appropriately on social media. In order for you to change your sexuality for the better, you will need to know the ins and outs of your sexuality.

The second guidepost is *accountability*. We are all individually liable for our sexual fulfillment, health, experience, and happiness. We do not rely on others to make us emotionally, physically, spiritually, or psychologically well. All too often we expect our partner to care take our sexuality even though we would never expect our partner to do so in any other dimension of our lives. If anything, we would be considered unhealthy if we were to do so. There are names for such unhealthy expectations: codependent, enabled, enmeshed, or riding the coat tails of another's faith.

Just as physical health is the responsibility of the individual struggling to exercise, lose weight, talk to their doctor, or otherwise, it is the responsibility of each person to advocate for their sexual health. When awareness of a biological or medical concern impacting sexuality is brought to the attention of the individual, for example, SAAM posits that the individual themselves need to advocate for sexual health improvement by ensuring the appropriate doctor visit. As it is brought to the attention of a client that sexual fantasy is lacking, where it has earlier in life produced sexual desire and sexual fulfillment, the individual self-advocates by fostering sexual fantasy and cultivating a sexual imagination. A partner can be a help and support, but the responsibility lies with the individual lacking fantasy.

SAAM uses elements of acceptance. At times client's expectations and hopes are not met because of unknowns, relational injuries and limitations, inflexible partners, physical limitations, needed medication, mental or physical illness, etc. An acceptance component to our model helps people to adapt, mourn loss or unmet needs, and find fulfillment and sexual health and happiness in their life and relationship. Through creating new expectations based off of realities, a couple can be at peace with their sex lives.

A few important insights about your voyage:

- Your raft or sexuality will go down the river or life, no matter if you choose to be on it, attentive and accountable, or not.
- Choose to be an active and present sailor on your raft.

- What type of sailor will you choose to be? A true sailor will be one with the raft and sea. A poor sailor will allow the raft or river to overcome.
- Problematic sexual behavior, hyper-sexuality, compulsive/impulsive sexual behavior, or addiction is letting the raft take over and becoming entangled with the sailor. May appear from too much attention to one's raft or sexuality.
- We lose our sexual identity when we abandon the raft, allow the river to erode away at the raft's integrity, or we fall into the river (get lost in life to the neglect of our sexuality).
- Sexual desire issues may come from too little attention to the raft
- Sexual dysfunction can come when we let the river take over.
- We become sexually weak when one spouse takes command of one's raft or we give our raft to our spouse.
- We sail ahead when our partner is not willing to come on the journey and when we ignore our partner. Be mindful of when it is healthy to be sexually differentiated and when you are neglecting your fleet. We are fleet-going sailors, but at times it's important to float at our pace and not lose our independence.

As this book progresses, I want you to continue to think of some of the things that your raft has been equipped with and some of the things that you have elected to bring on your raft. As always, I want you to think about the river; the river can swallow you up or give life. I have elected to only discuss in detail this model within this single chapter. References through the book will go back to SAAM, but I want you to otherwise filter the remainder of the book through this theoretical framework. For example, later on I discuss being in the moment and enjoying the pleasure that is present rather than evaluating whether or not the pleasure you feel is adequate or acceptable. This concept leads back to the systems within, specifically your psychology or personality characteristics. The model is therefore used throughout the book but not always explicitly. I hope you enjoy your sexual journey and the course I have helped to chart within this book.

LDS FAITH &
SEXUALITY

W ithin this chapter, I will address *my* understanding of the LDS Church's stance on marital sexuality, how cultural messages and interpretations can lead to sexual struggles, and shifts in thinking to answer disappointment and frustration. (As always, I include an activity at the end.) I want to begin by stating that my understanding concerning the LDS Church's beliefs about sexual intimacy is that the LDS Church is in full support of a healthy and satisfying sex life between husband and wife. In fact, while I was writing this book, the LDS Church published a short article for family home evening, "Sexual Intimacy is Sacred and Beautiful" (The Church of Jesus Christ of Latter-day Saints, 2017)). The Church references Ephesians 5:31 and goes on to discuss how sexual intimacy in marriage is vital to discuss on an ongoing basis with our children and that our gospel teaches that sexuality is a *powerful* gift from our Father in Heaven. When I speak of the LDS *culture*, I am in no way referring to the beliefs, opinions, teachings, or doctrines of the LDS Church. The culture is developed by the members of the LDS Church, *not* by the leaders. Culture can be helpful, neutral, or hurtful.

A few years back, my wife and I were called to team teach our ward's marital and family relations class. Who would have thought it? Two therapists . . . We were sitting ducks! In all seriousness, we were very excited to be teaching a course that was in line with what we did for our professions. Up until that point, I had never sat in on or taught the marital and family relations class, nor had my wife. Because of this, all of the material presented in this manner was new to us. Being a sex therapist, I can't begin to tell you how excited I was to read the chapter that contained teachings on marital intimacy. I was floored when I finished this chapter with my wife, and we began to talk about what we had just read and how we were going to present it to our class.

The Church had done an excellent job at presenting the marital sexual relationship in a magnificent light. There were two clear aspects that the church highlighted. The first was the aspect of procreation, and I'm sure you are well-aware of the importance that the church places on this topic. The second and *equally* stressed aspect was that of marital sex being a physical, emotional, and spiritual part of a satisfying and bonded marital relationship. There were several quotes from the brethren of the church that highlighted both aspects. I wanted to share some of the significant statements from leaders of the LDS Church concerning sexual intimacy in marriage. In my estimation, their message to married couples is twofold: marital sexual intimacy is for procreation and is an expression of love.

President Spencer W. Kimball taught, "In the context of lawful marriage, the intimacy of sexual relations is right and divinely approved. There is nothing unholy or degrading about sexuality in itself, for by that means men and women join in a process of creation and in an expression of love."[1]

Elder Jeffrey R. Holland of the Quorum of the Twelve Apostles taught,

> Human intimacy is reserved for a married couple because it is the ultimate symbol of total union, a totality and a union ordained and defined by God. From the Garden of Eden onward, marriage was intended to mean the complete merger of a man and a woman—their hearts, hopes, lives, love, family, future, everything. Adam said of Eve that she was bone of his bones and flesh of his flesh, and that they were to be "one flesh" in their life together [see Gen. 2:23–24]. This is a union of such completeness that we use the word seal to convey its eternal promise. The Prophet Joseph Smith once said we perhaps could render such a sacred bond as being "welded" one to another [see D&C 128:18].[2]

From a scientific point, I find this last statement incredibly fascinating since sexual expression in humans releases a chemical called oxytocin that literally bonds and connects individuals together. There have been fascinating studies that examine the mating habits of animals that produce oxytocin when mating; animals that produce such a chemical mate for life. They are "welded" together in a sense. When this chemical is blocked, the animals no longer mate for life. In that way, intercourse "welds" and bonds these two creatures together.

Despite these quotes and other countless attempts that I'm sure are made by the LDS Church, some of the culture within the LDS faith send a far different message. Because I am a therapist who works with couples who struggle in their sexual relationships, you can imagine the kinds of stories I hear about the lack of sexual education, the inaccurate portrayal of sex, or the misinformation that both men and women have received from parents, loved ones, friends, and even leaders all throughout their lives. Some of these messages have been lifelong, existed throughout marriage, been engendered right before the wedding night, or grown over the course of the first years of marriage.

Although I was prepared to hear of appalling or unbelievable stories from clients, I'm still flabbergasted at the thought that these men and women weren't informed, were poorly informed, or were misinformed. I can still remember the first time a client shared with me that her parents told her that the marital sexual relationship was just for the man and that the woman doesn't and won't get anything out of it. I stress the "first time" part because I have sadly heard this horrific story more than once. To set the story straight, sexual relationships are equally important for *both* partners. Women have every right and privilege to enjoy all aspects of a sexual relationship, just as men do. I know of many women who sincerely do.

This was a point I had to stress to a former client. Jane had, until the beginning of therapy, no sexual desire whatsoever to her recollection. She was also unable to orgasm. When she was told that she had every right and privilege to enjoy a sexual relationship with Joey, it was eye-opening to her. This appears obvious. However, having it stated out loud so clearly pinpointed that she had felt the contrary was true all of her life, and it was truly a new concept to her. Jane thought about this over the course of the next few weeks. Upon a subsequent visit, she discussed her newfound satisfaction in her sex life and her ability to have an orgasm during sex. Jane previously had no enjoyment during sex, and now she was able to orgasm and, more importantly, longed for sexual intimacy.

Needless to say, this transition in thinking set in motion a process that was life-changing. She highlighted the aforementioned concept as a game changer for her and as what brought her to the right mental place to allow orgasm to happen. She said, "Your words that I deserve to have a satisfying sexual experience just as much as any man rang in my mind since we met last." As Jane thought about this, her self-concept shifted dramatically. She went from viewing herself as a woman who hadn't ever had any sexual desire and who wasn't sexual to viewing herself as a woman who had as much sexual potential as anyone else. Jane's new view altered how she thought about herself throughout the day while away from Joey and while they were spending time together emotionally and sexually, triggering more avenues for her to move to sexual intimacy and ultimately orgasm.

I cannot overstate the importance of culture on sexual functioning. I would say that a large majority of the cases that I work with have some sort of cultural tie-in to the problem. There are countless examples of how conservative cultures, like the LDS culture, have engendered sexual issues. I have such examples, as you do, and there are numerous others that you can find in books, blogs, and the like. It's almost needless to say that there is a dire need for a cultural adjustment regarding the view of sexuality and the way in which it is addressed in our lives. Oftentimes these negative messages are conveyed without words.

If you have been a victim of cultural sexual negativity or misguided information, it is up to you to accurately educate yourself. No one will do this for you; you must advocate for yourself. What better way to not be a victim than by becoming a survivor? Survivors do not live by the messages they receive. They own their sexuality, see themselves as sexual beings, counter the inaccurate messages with truth, and embrace the sexual desire and arousal they feel. At times, it requires work. However, it's very rewarding work. This can come by way of seeking out actual LDS leadership views of marital sexuality as described in statements such as the above, reading books (such as this one) that correct inaccurate misattributions, and beginning to talk to those who are safe and who you trust (not easy, but very worthwhile). Lastly, you should discontinue perpetuating these negative cultural messages. I see the LDS Church doing a tremendous job in bringing about a cultural shift in the view of marital sexuality.

◈ MINI-ACTIVITY ◈

Take a brief break from reading to post on social media something that is sex positive. Extra points to those that find something that ties religion to sex positive messages. You can provide a link to an article, website, blog, or book if you aren't as eloquent as you'd like. This will reverberate in our culture and shift the way that we as a people think about sex.

I want to talk a little about the dramatic shift in implicit/explicit messages of "thou shall not" to "thou shall, and often." Couples frequently bring this topic up in therapy, and rightfully so. They have been taught all of their lives that they should not engage in sexual intercourse or any sexual activity until marriage. A dramatic shift then occurs after the couple kneels across the altar and makes covenants to each other and God. This is not an easy shift to embrace or to sustain. Typically, they feel the transformative message sink in during their reception or on the way to their honeymoon suite. They either have tried or have been successful at staying morally clean for all these years.

Once they are married, however, those things that they have tried to steer clear from are available possibilities. Not only are they in the realm of possibility, but they are also they are strongly encouraged. Even more, the larger society teaches that men are to be Casanovas by nature. This only adds to the immense pressure men feel to perform and be "good" at sex once they are married. It additionally misrepresents the female role in their sexual relationship. Females are wrongly taught that they are the recipient of sexuality and created sexual only by their sexually competent male partner rather than shouldering the responsibility for their own sexuality and expression. These newlywed LDS couples are taught that they need to have a regular and fulfilling sexual relationship, but they typically don't have the experience, knowledge, and mindset to get started.

It is heartbreaking to hear these strong Latter-day Saints shake in their testimonies due to the issues in their sexual relationships. Some have expressed resentment toward God or their way of life because they experience pain, low sexual desire, inability to orgasm, premature ejaculation, erectile dysfunction, or a low level of sexual satisfaction during what should be highly pleasurable and bonding sexual relationships with their spouses. I want to make clear that I am in full support of the church, that men and women should stay morally clean prior to marriage. However, this doesn't mean that they won't and don't experience some difficulty in transitioning once sex is condoned and encouraged.

I have found it helpful for couples experiencing difficulty during this transition phase to think of their single lives as a chapter in the book of their lives, one where they didn't entertain sexual thoughts and fantasies, where they did not encourage sexuality, where they were morally clean and pure, and where they were excited to one day have a sexual relationship and enjoy being touched as well as touching their partner. When they enter into the covenant of marriage, they can then enter a new chapter of their lives. In this chapter, they can grow thoughts, actions, and feelings that were not encouraged before. Within this new chapter of their lives, they can explore with their spouses those things that feel good sexually. They can contemplate themselves as sexual beings with sexual urges and desires that they now get to explore. They can investigate what these urges and desires might be because they have chosen to refrain from active engagement in the previous chapters of their lives. They can embrace their physical form as sexual and erotic with highly embedded sexual capacities. They can fantasize and think about sexual intimacy while their spouses are away. They can build excitement about new sexual touches and experiences that will happen when their spouses return or during their next sexual encounter.

This new chapter includes a lot of deliberate effort to transform into a being who is sexual and who sees this as a very important component of their entire person. This is a journey, since suppressing these feelings and urges for all their single years and then embracing them can be, for some, a mighty challenge. Remember on your journey that the sexual relationship that exists between husband and wife is one of the truly unique aspects of marriage that sets it apart from any other relationship.[3] This should be celebrated.

Claire and Ryan were as excited as could be to get married and finally share in a sexual relationship within the covenant of marriage. They had spent all their lives being as virtuous as possible. They had some slip-ups along the way, but were mostly steadfast in holding to strict morality. They were excited to have sex and enjoy this God-given act within the sacred bonds of marriage, since it hadn't always been easy over their single lives. The wedding night was filled with enthusiasm as the couple drove to their hotel in Salt Lake City and checked in. Once in their room, the couple found that sex wasn't as easy as they thought it would be. Ryan was able to get a firm erection, but Claire experienced some discomfort as they tried penetration. Using a lubricant helped some, but Claire was in pain by the time that Ryan began thrusting. Trying to reduce the pain Claire felt and shifting positions reduced the rigidity of Ryan's penis, and he soon lost his erection. The couple was tired, frustrated, and let down that their years of high moral character resulted in a honeymoon night that was significantly subpar.

Over the course of the next year, the couple put a great deal of effort into enhancing their sexual relationship. While sex wasn't always painful, Claire found that it was only rarely pleasant. It was at this point that Claire and Ryan found themselves sitting in my office. What finally helped this couple find real satisfaction within their sexual relationship was viewing Claire's single and married life in distinct chapters. Claire ended therapy with a different concept of this married chapter of her life. One example of how she was able to do this was in her appraisal and view of her body. She found herself looking at her naked body in a sexual way. Not only was her body God-given as the single chapter of her life taught her, but it was also designed to be sexually arousing and sexually responsive. She found certain parts of her body were more erotic, and enjoyed Ryan touching these parts and imagining this touch when the two were apart from each other. This and many parallel shifts in thinking engendered more arousal during foreplay, which brought about the needed anatomical shifts in the vaginal canal requisite for pain-free sex.

It is a nice thought that couples who abstain from engaging in sexual behaviors prior to marriage would then be able to transition into a marital sexual relationship with ease. However, this is just not the case. The old adage that anything worth doing in life takes practice is very much applicable to sexual relationships. I will not negate the possible feelings of frustration and aggravation that accompany issues in your marital sexual relationship when you have been faithful or tried to be so during your single life. However, I will say that some of the issues that couples face may just require adaptability and practice. I want to provide you an example of what I am describing.

Calvin struggled with erectile dysfunction. His wife, Amy, didn't want to attend therapy, but she also had sexual dysfunction. She was unable to have an orgasm. Calvin and Amy had only been married two years, but had already felt the relational impact of their sexual challenges. While Calvin and I did work on resolving his erectile dysfunction, I only want to focus here on Amy's anorgasmia. Calvin was discouraged, as Amy had pretty much given up on being able to have an orgasm. She was really discouraged and upset over this and was willing to accept that she might never be able to achieve orgasm. Being the optimist and proponent for sexual fulfillment that I am, I wasn't willing to allow her discouragement to rob them of this experience.

Calvin and Amy had an otherwise great relationship. At the close of one of our sessions, I provided Calvin with some references to church leaders concerning sexual intimacy. I also encouraged him to dispel some of Amy's sexual myths about women and encouraged the couple to continue to try to provide her with sexual pleasure instead of just giving up. Within the next two weeks, Amy had an orgasm. Not just one, but several. Her hang-up was the discouragement that she felt after getting married and finding that sex wasn't as easy as she thought. This, for her, was evidence that sex wasn't for her as a woman, as she had been told her whole life. A little psychological education and a clearer religious understanding provided her with all that she needed to adapt and become orgasmic.

Now these are quick results. You may have the same results as this couple; more often than not, it takes a while longer. However, what could possibly be more fun than practicing sexual intimacy or working toward a more fulfilling sexual relationship with your spouse?

What I propose to my clients and to you is a paradigm shift. Yes, it is undeniable that you are experiencing highly unfavorable sexual circumstances. I commiserate with each of you. However, you have the unique ability to experience for the first time, or for the first time in the right context, a godly, intimate relationship with one another. You get to explore your own and your partner's sexuality in a covenant marriage, the most holy of circumstances. You get to educate, adapt, grow, and flourish sexually as a couple sealed in God's holy temple. To me, that makes up for the trials that you will face.

These trials also deserve a shift in thinking. Instead of viewing the sexual struggles as a horrific issue that creates a wedge within the marriage, start seeing the sexual struggle as an opportunity for you as a couple to learn, adapt, grow, and flourish sexually and intimately. When on the same team, and with the approach and tenets set out in this book, you will not fail. God has given you a special gift in laying out sexual guidelines for your pre- and post-marital life. He has provided you the gift of creating a sexual culture, understanding, and experience that is not sullied by past experiences and is uniquely yours as a couple. How fortunate you are. To illustrate this shift, below is an example from therapy.

Megan and Steve presented in therapy with complaints of sexual pain. They had been married a year, been to medical doctors, and tried to resolve these issues on their own, but to no avail. They were still unable to have sex without it being very painful for Megan. As I worked with them in therapy, I could see that several needed shifts in thinking were required. The couple was encouraged to see this as an exciting process that they, as a couple sealed in God's holy temple, could embark on. Megan was encouraged to see this as a new chapter in her life, where she was a sexual being created in such a way that fulfilling her divine potential meant fostering a sexual sense of self. Lastly, she was to let go of any expectations that she was supposed to feel a certain amount of sexual desire or pleasure and to be in the moment during intimacy and to feel whatever desire was present without expectations.

With time, Megan and Steve made the shift from dismay and discouragement to excitement as they embarked on this fun journey. Megan was able to let go of any expectation for how she should feel and, because of this, was able to allow in some sexual thoughts that she had put off in the single chapter of her life. She began thinking more about sex and seeing herself as a sexual being both with her partner and alone. Not too long into therapy, she came up with some scenarios that she thought were sexually arousing. They were then able to make some breakthroughs in treatment. They could progress through the activities given, and she found satisfaction in sex with the absence of pain. This was due in large part to the couple's adaptability in changing negative perceptions into positive ones.

One of the best ways for you and your spouse to start your marriage is by educating yourself and your partner about what turns you on and increases your satisfaction or pleasure. Next, you need to communicate and show this to your partner. This doesn't make you a selfish lover or an inappropriate lover. It just makes you someone who knows what he or she wants and knows how to communicate it. If anything, you are doing your partner a disservice by not being more forthright. You are robbing your partner of a more satisfying and pleasurable experience for you both, as he or she will find your increased arousal to be the largest aphrodisiac imaginable. In essence, you are expecting your spouse to read your mind or hoping that he or she will happen upon whatever it is that pleases you.

This is irrational thinking and needs to be rectified, especially if you are unaware of what arouses you. How is your spouse supposed to know if you yourself haven't a clue?

I have found that many of my couple clients fall within this category. I would say that it is more normal than atypical for couples I have met with. So don't get down on yourself or your partner. I am more often surprised by those couples who figure out that they need to know what feels good for them and then communicate this in some fashion to their partners. Our culture, and really the larger society in which we live, strongly portrays that once we begin a sexual encounter we will figure it out. How can we without a little, or a lot, of communication between the couple, especially if you have never had sex with anyone in the past? How exciting! We get to know ourselves and then communicate and show this to our spouses.

Cindy and Victor were a young couple who presented in therapy because Cindy was very unaware of her sexual preferences. She was in large part disgusted or turned off by her own sexual anatomy and functioning. Cindy would at times be able to orgasm, other times she experienced pain during intercourse, and other encounters varied greatly. She didn't know for herself what would cause any of these responses. Her husband, Victor, was similarly perplexed, and they had seen many medical doctors and tried everything they could think of before coming to therapy. Due to her unawareness, Cindy wasn't able to communicate any sexual preferences to Victor. He was lost as far as what direction to go to help. Through activities similar to those described in this section, Cindy was able to identify what was arousing to her and communicate this to Victor. Sex soon became less of an unknown and became more enjoyable for both partners. This is a classic example of how the lack of sexual self-awareness can lead to sexual dissatisfaction and sexual dysfunction.

I was recently on a trip with my wife to San Diego. I have been there before, but never before had I experienced this city in quite the same way. Perhaps it was because I was writing this book that my experience differed more than in times past. I noticed myself relaxing into my skin more than at any other time in my life. I took particular note of this. As an aside, these are the musings that take place in the mind of a therapist while he's on vacation. I observed that there was no pressure to be or act any certain way. I experienced no judgment, but only acceptance. If anything, difference was celebrated. I typically felt the pressure to be or act a certain way while growing up in Utah and more so around the LDS culture, but I hadn't really noticed how it may be different anywhere else. I think that sexuality in our culture can at times be this way. There is a pressure or expectation that we need to be or act sexually in a particular way or else we fear that we are doing something wrong, strange, obscure, out of the norm, or are judged. This limits the myriad ways that individuals experience sexuality and express it.

Part of this expectation, I'm sure, is derived from the limited sexual experiences that many of us have had or are talking about and sharing with each other. Thus, we grow to have a more limited knowledge about what constitutes sexuality as men or women experience it instead of a more accepting understanding that sexuality and its expression are as different and varied as the clothing adorned on my trip to San Diego. These residents expressed their style in a way that was congruent to them and had no shame for it. Our sexuality needs to be expressed in a congruent fashion with no regard for the "norm" and our individuality needs to be celebrated by self and spouse. This mindset validates our experience and takes away expectation and pressure to be a certain way sexually. By being able to express our sexuality as we see fit, we stand to gain more desire and pleasure.

ᴀ *ACTIVITY* ᴀ

As stated at the beginning of this book, it is important that the couple counsel together, discover what is within their value systems, and adhere to those activities. You can modify all of these activities or begin at various progressive steps. Just take into account the pitfalls that may befall you when doing so.

The activity for this section is enormously effective. It is also the building block for the activity in the subsequent chapter. It begins as an individual activity for both husband and wife and then progresses to a couple's activity. This is a standard sex therapy activity that I prescribe to almost all couples who come to therapy for issues of sexual desire, arousal, orgasm, pain, and satisfaction. I'll go into detail and then discuss some apprehensions that I have experienced from some LDS couples and what we have determined would make them feel they are operating within their value systems.

This first step is purely educational and confidence building. None of these initial assignments are meant to be sexual in nature. If you find them arousing or find that they increase sexual desire, do not stop. Take note of this and discuss it with your spouse afterward. Finding this activity sexual is neither good nor bad. Ignoring or not allowing pleasure in it is bad. So is it similar if you feel uncomfortable or weird about examining your sexual anatomy. The first activity is for each spouse to explore and identify his or her external sexual anatomy. It is important that we understand all parts of our God-given bodies. For instance, you know your hands well and can use them to the best of their abilities. If you never developed this knowledge and understanding as a baby and child, you would be limited in their functionality. Likewise, if you do not learn your sexual anatomy, you can be limited in capability. Men may find this activity to be quick. Take a little more time to examine subtle characteristics that you may have overlooked throughout your life. Each partner alone should find a setting where you can relax and not be disturbed. Eliminate any time constraints so that you can be in the moment and perform the exercise without such constraints pulling you out of the activity. Women especially may find that music, dim lights, or doing this exercise while no one else is in the house is the best setting to relax and not be distracted. Women may need a mirror to see sexual anatomy more easily. Each partner is to look at a medical drawing or picture of sexual anatomy and identify on his or her own body the corresponding sexual anatomy. This diagram can be found at covenantsextherapy.com. Woman should identify and explore the labia majora, labia minora, clitoral hood, clitoris, and vaginal opening. Men should identify and explore the glans, shaft, scrotum, and testicles. The first purpose of this exercise is for each spouse to find that you have all of the necessary sexual anatomy to enjoy sexual intercourse. Notation of more than that such parts merely exist is encouraged and what will make this exercise truly effective. We will discuss this further a little later. If something feels arousing you can explore what is making it so and then store that information so that you can teach your spouse. Each of us is uniquely made by God. Please enjoy seeing how uniquely, majestically, and beautifully He has created you. By the way, that is how you need to start seeing yourself. Anything otherwise will negatively impact your sexual functioning.

Now that you are familiar with the essential sexual anatomy of your body, I want you to share your knowledge with your spouse. Please share with him or her by way of showing your spouse your uniquely designed and created body. You may feel that you and your spouse have been married for twenty years and know each others' bodies very intimately and that this exercise is useless. If that is your thinking, I want you to consider how often your spouse has shown you his or her anatomy in a nonsexual way without performance pressure. How often have you engaged in any nonsexual act that increased both partners' comfort with your own and your partner's sexual anatomy and that helped honor and cherish your unique sexual anatomies? How often have these nonsexual experiments increased your or your partner's comfort in knowledge and teaching about his or her body? How often are you truly trying to understand each others' bodies in a way that is unselfish? My educated guess is not very often.

For the sake of ease, I will phrase the remainder of the activity directed at the wife with her spouse learning and implementing this knowledge. However, I intend that each spouse will go through this similar process. For the next step, the wife is then asked to touch her sexual anatomy with various intensities or kinds of touch and to explore what is pleasurable and with what kind of touch. It is very important that she understands that this assignment isn't for her to have an orgasm or to go through all of the phases of the sexual response cycle. This step is for her to find what parts of her sexual anatomy are pleasurable to touch, with what type of touch, and how to increase pleasure. It is important that she understands that this is not an assignment to masturbate. This is needed insight to bring into the martial relationship. This is particularly liberating for women. In our society, there is more priority placed on how women look than on a knowledge of their own body.

After the wife is aware of her own sexual anatomy and what parts of this anatomy feel good and with what touch, she is then able to advocate for herself and communicate this to her husband, which is the next step of the activity. In this step, each partner is to show their spouse which parts of their sexual anatomy are pleasurable to touch, what kinds of touch they enjoy, and how much intensity to use. To do this, show your partner through self-touch what feels pleasurable to you. Next, you can place your partner's hand on your own and have him or her shadow your movement as you touch yourself. Allow the partner showing what touch is pleasurable to be in complete control. You are to simply watch, keep your hand on top of your spouse's, and learn. Next, your hand will be touching your partner's genitalia with his or her hand on top of yours directing your touch. For example, if the wife's vulva is being touched, her husband will place his hand directly on her vulva. She will then place her hand on top of his and guide his touch. She will go through the entire process of building arousal so that he can feel what changes take place with her genitalia and what aims her various movements are trying to reach. The husband will see and feel firsthand what anatomy is desirable to touch and how his wife would like to be touched as her arousal increases. This process is still entirely in the control of the wife.

Whenever I assign this activity to a couple, I ensure that each feels comfortable doing this activity and that it fits within his or her value system. The positive impact of the activity will most likely be hindered if the woman isn't able to relax because she feels bad or guilty for doing the assignment or vice versa. I have found that women who fall within this camp are more comfortable with their spouses either being present in the room (also touching their own sexual anatomy) or being the one doing the touching of the woman. All of these are good first-step alternatives and are definitely better than neglecting the activity.

I will tell you what I tell all of my clients. I don't want you to simply do this activity because I as a professional told you to but because you feel comfortable and want to do the activity. If you do not feel that this assignment falls within your value system, and if one of the alternatives I previously mentioned would be more suitable to you, then we can work with that. One of the reasons that sex therapy literature prescribes your partner to be absent is because solo exploration eliminates spectatorship. Having your spouse in the room for part of your assignment can present some roadblocks, such as feeling some need to perform, awareness that another person is watching what you are doing, or feelings to rush or hurry, all of which prevent you from relaxing and exploring for as long as you need. After these roadblocks are explored, the couple can investigate how these roadblocks can be avoided while still performing the activity within their value systems.

In the space below, write down what you have learned from the activity. What did you find? Are you discovering pleasure that was never there before? If so, describe this pleasure. Maybe you are struggling to feel okay about what you are doing. Explore this with you partner and write down your thoughts and feelings. What was it like when your partner was in the room and shadowing?

_____

_____

_____

_____

_____

_____

_____

_____

_____

_____

*What do you need to be **attentive** to from this chapter?*

_____

_____

*What do you need to be **accountable** for from this chapter?*

_____

_____

*What do you need to **accept** about this chapter?*

_____

_____

*What needs to be **re-storied** from this chapter?*

_____

_____

❧ NOTES ❧

1. Spencer W. Kimball in Edward Kimball, ed., *The Teachings of Spencer W. Kimball* (Salt Lake City: Deseret Book, 1982), 311.
2. Jeffrey R. Holland, "Personal Purity," *Ensign*, November 1998, 76.
3. See Dean M. Busby, Jason S. Carroll, and Chelom Leavitt, *Sexual Wholeness in Marriage: An LDS Perspective on Integrating Sexuality and Spirituality in Our Marriages* (United States of America: Book Printers of Utah, 2013).

SEXUAL
EDUCATION

T his chapter will provide you with the basics of sexual education.
A basic understanding is all that you need on a practical level to
have a fulfilling sex life with your partner. I will go over both
male and female sexual anatomy, as pertinent to a couple's sexual relationship. We will then focus on the sexual response cycle for both genders.

Concepts in this chapter are important, as I will refer back to sexual
anatomy and the sexual response cycle stages throughout the book. Men,
don't tune out or skip over the women's section; vice versa for women.
You need to know about each others' anatomy and how your partner's
body works. A full sexual experience requires knowledge of your partner.
Without this, you are robbing yourself and your partner of a more satisfying experience.

We are trying to break the mold of what your culture and larger society might have taught you about sex and, more globally, intimacy. Your
and your partner's sexual anatomies and functionalities are magnificent
and beautiful. Also, accurate terms are a must. I want to make sure that
you, your partner, and I are all on the same page when discussing something as crucial as your sexual relationship.

I want to start out by saying that men and women are more alike than
we are dissimilar when it comes to our sexual organs. That may sound
strange, but I think that you will agree as I discuss male and female sexual
organ formation. You will most likely recall some of this from middle

school or junior high biology or sexual education courses, though you may have chosen to block it out.

All human beings form their sexual organs from the same starting point—what are called prenatal homologous structures. As the fetus develops, these prenatal homologous structures form into either male or female sexual anatomy. For the male, there develops the glans penis, urethral folds, and labioscrotal swelling. The female develops the glans clitoris, urethral folds, and labioscrotal swelling. As the stages of sexual development continue, the male develops scrotal swelling that turns into the scrotum with testes, and the female develops the labia majora and minora, or lips of the vagina. There are other features unique to male and female sexual anatomies that also occur, but the above are most significant for our purposes. Please look with your spouse at the prenatal homologous structures and then pull up the medical anatomy of an adult man and woman. You can easily access pictures of these online from my website at covenantsextherapy.com.

A few years ago, a couple disclosed to me that they were unsure if Tiffany, the wife, had a clitoris. I prescribed the two of them an activity, along with an associated medical drawing of the female sexual anatomy, to examine their own and then their partner's sexual anatomy. Upon returning to therapy, Michael and Tiffany were still unsure if what they identified as the clitoris was in fact correct. It appeared to feel quite different from the other parts of the vulva and was located where the clitoris should be, but they couldn't see a distinct structure. This was highly important for the couple, as Tiffany struggled with getting sexually aroused and couldn't achieve climax. They were referred to a medical doctor who was able to point out the clitoris and answer the question that was weighing in their minds. It turned out that Tiffany's clitoris was concealed with vulva tissue that hid its appearance. After the confusion was cleared up, Tiffany more easily relaxed and enjoyed sexual touch from Michael, knowing that there wasn't anything wrong with her body. Not surprisingly, she was more aroused with the same kind of touch that he had provided many times prior simply by knowing that he was rubbing her clitoris. Tiffany enjoyed that it was an erotic sexual structure that she had heard sexualized by many of her friends. Additionally, Tiffany felt more arousal from manual, oral, and penetrative sex as the couple could focus sexual contact for her on her clitoris. The narratives that we ascribe to can be transformative to our experience and, in this case, satisfaction.

It is interesting to note that the clitoris has only one function for women, which is to provide pleasure. It is covered with twice as many nerve endings as the head of a man's penis as well. The clitoris is quite a bit smaller than the head of the penis. What a magnificent gift. So for those women who have come to believe that sex is just for men, think again.

A while back I worked with a seasoned wife who impressed me, because she did not take for granted the sexual capacity that was afforded her as a daughter of God made with unique aptitude for sexual pleasure. Mariana had been a sexual woman for as long as she could remember. She never acted on her sexual desire when single, but capitalized on this once she and Simon had married seventeen years earlier. She greatly enjoyed sexual intimacy and reveled in anticipation of the next time that she and Simon would have a chance, after the kids were in bed, to have sex. Mariana's ability to accept her body as one with high sexual ability served the couple well. She viewed herself as an equal in sexual competence to Simon by knowing that her body included the creation of a clitoris with great ability for pleasure. This knowledge and acceptance, along with excitement in exploration at the formative years of their relationship, set the stage for Mariana to develop into the sexual giant that I was fortunate to meet with.

There are a few important points to make concerning each gender at the onset of this section. With men, the pre-ejaculate, or what is often referred to as pre-cum, can get the woman pregnant. Nocturnal emissions are often referred to as wet dreams and are common for men to experience. While asleep and awake, it is important for men to experience erection, as the blood flow is requisite to keep the penis vital. Men will often feel as though they want to have sex in the morning, although an erection might only be due to this normal, vital process. Desire is an imperative piece of sexuality and may be absent if sex is sought after simply because an erection is present.

Our society often refers to the exterior of the woman's genitalia as the vagina instead of the correct term, vulva. The vagina is the internal barrel-like structure of the female sexual anatomy. The clitoris is often an afterthought and not seen as an important structure, although it is extremely crucial for sexual functioning. As vasocongestion occurs, blood flows to the vulva, resulting in increased size or tone to the labia, which can augment generalized arousal to the vulva and clitoris.

It is important for every couple to understand the sexual response cycle (SRC). At the beginning stages of worldly knowledge of human sexuality, it was initially understood that the SRC was the same for men and women. This cycle was seen as linear and graduated. That is, men and women start with being aroused and then move to orgasm followed by resolution, as found by Dr. Masters and Virginia Johnson (Masters and Johnson, 1966). This graduated model has clear, stepwise progression from one stage of the sexual response cycle to another. Another researcher along the way, Dr. Helen Singer Kaplan, made an important distinction to the aforementioned SRC. She added sexual desire as a precursor (Kaplan, 1983). Desire has since been a relevant piece in the SRC. I think that many still thank her for this addition.

Some women reading this may feel that these models are more closely related to how men experience sex than how women do. Well, they are correct. You are not the only one astute enough to notice this bias. A researcher named Dr. Rosemary Basson challenged these linear approaches by providing a female SRC that was nonlinear and incorporated components of emotional intimacy, sexual stimulus, and relationship satisfaction (Basson, 2000). Thus, biological functioning is not the focus of a woman's SRC, as it is in the linear approach.

Another hallmark of Basson's model is that women can be receptive, or make a decision to be aroused or to be open to arousal (Basson, 2000). I want to make sure this point sinks in, so I will repeat it. Women often make a choice to allow sexual desire and arousal, instead of acting or not acting upon whatever they physically/emotionally feel in the moment, as is stereotypical with men. This is a much more sophisticated approach. Women exhibit a superior form of functioning than the stereotypical male-reactive mode of functioning (i.e., "I feel aroused; therefore, I seek out intercourse.").

I want all of you women to think about this for a moment. Think of a time you had sex when it was earth-shattering. I'm guessing that there was a point at which you made a conscious decision to be sexual, allow arousal, accept touch as erotic, or transition into a sexual mode. Further, this decision was most likely profound in transforming the sexual encounter to a highly pleasurable event. Now communicate this process to your partner. He can learn something about your higher functionality. This nonlinear approach, which takes into account the couple's relationship as well as has more diffuse boundaries from one phase to another, has been accepted as the gold standard and is now used in the new *Diagnostic and Statistical Manual* for mental health professionals.

Basson's model is a lot more complex in nature than the aforementioned models. As I have worked in the field of sexuality, I have found that many men also fit within this more complex model. In fact, the idea that "a sexual encounter needs to progress or else the sexual encounter is failing" puts the man in a very vulnerable state where he can allow his thought processes to decrease his arousal. That is, thinking that his body is responding unfavorably or out of the male norm, he allows negative thoughts about his sexual capability to take over and decrease his confidence in having the firm erection that is necessary for intercourse, thus leading to erectile dysfunction, for example. Instead, if the man were able to see that his SRC is similar to that of the woman's—where it is normal for him to jump around in the phases of the SRC—then his negative thoughts wouldn't be present and wouldn't be capable of taking him out of the moment. He could think, "Oh, my erection is softening, and this is the normal ebb and flow of the SRC. I'm excited for the process of it slowly becoming erect again. It feels good when it's growing." He could then focus on other arousing touches or movements and on enjoying the process of a returning erection.

Rex was the perfect example of the detrimental impact that the inaccurate perception of sexual functioning can have on a man. He and Liz had been married almost two years, and they hadn't been able to have intercourse. Rex had, on several occasions, lost his erection during foreplay over the first month of marriage. This really shouldn't have been anything to concern the couple, but they didn't realize this at the time. Rex built up some anxiety about keeping an erection and liked to stick to what he knew would keep him erect and what he knew would lead him to orgasm. So the couple spent nearly two years engaging in foreplay that ended in both partners climaxing as the sole method of their sexual relationship. Intercourse was off the table for the couple for the entire two years prior to treatment. They both wanted a change, but Rex was anxious that he would lose his erection during intercourse, which would obliterate his self-esteem. Liz was more than ready to try sex, but didn't want to rush Rex into doing something that he was uncomfortable with. Had Rex received realistic messages about the nature of the nonlinear SRC, he wouldn't have paid much attention to the formative experiences where he lost his erection, thus allowing him to enjoy regaining his erection, which would have certainly led to intercourse and the creation of a healthy sexual self-concept. You'll be happy to know that Rex and Liz have been able to have intercourse and now have two children.

Women benefit in a multiplicity of ways in seeing the SRC nonlinearly and specifically seeing there is ebb and flow to arousal. This places them in more control of their sexuality than the linear model. Similar to men, and perhaps more of a factor for women than men, a nonlinear model encourages instead of hinders female sexual functioning. When a woman is able to see that going from high sexual arousal to desire with minimal arousal isn't out of the norm, it makes it easier for her to go back to high arousal and orgasm. The woman is expecting something that is realistic and not expecting the misconceptions passed on through media and society, which allows her to enjoy the buildup of arousal throughout the sexual experience. When she can think of her sexual responses as typical for women, she can stay in the moment and enjoy the ebb and flow that facilitates more sexual arousal. Thus, her thoughts are able to stay in the sexual encounter instead of jumping to the undesirable, "I lost it. What's wrong with me? I bet there aren't many other women like this. I'm not sure if I'll be able to get aroused enough for an orgasm. I might as well just let my partner have an orgasm and then stop."

Another component of Basson's model of the SRC is that the goal of sexual intimacy is sexual satisfaction or pleasure—not orgasm (or even intercourse for that matter). Having the goal of orgasm produces lots of undesirable outcomes. When an individual or a couple is thinking that they need or their partner needs to have an orgasm for it to be successful, it can lead to performance anxiety and spectatorship. Both are highly correlated with sexual dissatisfaction. The focus of sex shifts from pleasure and being in the moment to reaching an orgasm and not being in the moment or enjoying the process. Thinking "Will I have or reach an orgasm?" isn't pleasurable and will most likely not lead to orgasm. Thinking "that touch, movement, closeness, warmth feels good—I want more of that" is pleasurable and may likely lead to orgasm. Whether orgasm happens or not, sex becomes enjoyable with this second way of thinking. When you think about it, the main purpose of having an orgasm, outside of procreation, is for a large amount of pleasure. So, if you are focusing on how pleasurable sexual intimacy is from the start and your entire goal is to increase pleasure, you will never be let down with this second way of thinking.

I want to cover the basic points of each phase of the SRC. As mentioned before, more understanding and literature is pointing to the blend of these phases. However, I believe it will be easier for you to hear about these phases as distinct from one another. Please keep in mind that this is for the sake of ease of explanation and that the phases really do blend with each other. The SRC phases of desire, arousal, orgasm, and resolution for both men and women will be covered below.

Sexual Response Cycle
Desire in Women

The female desire phase is characterized by the importance of high relationship quality. If the couple's relationship is satisfactory, then the wife is more likely to experience higher sexual desire for her spouse. Just as discussed in Basson's model, she is able to increase sexual desire for her husband when she spends more time thinking romantic or fond thoughts about her husband. Her desire is likely to be present within the context of the aforementioned and when she has a greater need to feel close to her spouse. Her sexual desire varies in longevity. She is likely to experience desire for anywhere from a few seconds to multiple days. Women are also more capable of easily suppressing their sexual desire than men are. This is more likely to happen when she feels a lack of love from her spouse or a lack of high relationship quality. Therefore, women have a more emotional aspect to their desire that is greatly influenced by their attitudes concerning the relationship and their partners. Basson argues that women make a conscious decision to proceed to arousal. Do not miss the critical decision-making point. Otherwise sex will be subpar. Additionally, Basson also states that sexual satisfaction comes from myriad contextual variables like relationship quality, stress, fulfillment, or feeling understood.

Sexual Response Cycle
Arousal/Excitement in Women

The female arousal/excitement phase, unlike the desire phase, is largely biological in nature. Heart and breathing rates increase during this phase. Swelling of the breasts, clitoris, and labia occur, which is called vasocongestion. This means that blood is pooling to these areas. The clitoris becomes like a miniature penis; as it fills with blood, it extends and pro-trudes from the clitoral hood that typically protects it, thus increasing sensitivity, which is usually desired at this phase. Interestingly, the clitoris is actually a lot larger than it may appear. The clitoris that you can see with the naked eye is only one tenth of the actual size of the clitoris (Roach, 2009). The rest is located internally and can be stimulated through the vaginal canal with "a come hither" hand motion. What is termed sexual flush takes place, where the development of pinkish spots occur, as well as darkening of the clitoris. The woman will notice that her vagina is beginning to lubricate, which is typically the key indicator of the arousal or excitement phase. Many of the other signs are subtler. Lots of women who are not in tune with their bodies, or who are taught not to be in tune with their bodies, don't know when they are sexually aroused. Male anatomy is a lot clearer about the presence of sexual arousal or excitement, as men have an erection that protrudes from their body. Exterior genitals make for ease of understanding. The woman's uterus also pulls up and away from the vagina at this point. The cervix also pulls up from the vagina. A visual of the interior of the vagina would show that the inner two-thirds of the vagina lengthens and distends, which makes it easier for intercourse. Therefore, if the woman is having a difficult time feeling aroused, intercourse can be uncomfortable or not as pleasing. This phase usually lasts anywhere from fifteen seconds to thirty minutes for women.

SEXUAL RESPONSE CYCLE PLATEAU IN WOMEN

The female plateau phase is also called the foreplay or love play stage. More of what happens in the arousal/excitement phase also happens in this stage. The uterus continues to elevate, the vaginal barrel expands, and the vagina continues to lubricate. The labia increase in size, muscle tension increases, and the clitoris retracts (due to the sensitivity of the cli-toris). This phase can be achieved, lost, and regained several times, which is all a normal part of the SRC for women. Women shouldn't let the loss of this phase dampen their spirits. Going with the wave or ebb of pleasure and allowing themselves to experience and enjoy whatever pleasure they feel will enable the plateau phase to return without negative thoughts preventing the return. The end of the plateau phase is when the woman reaches the moment of orgasmic inevitability; this is when an orgasm is going to occur no matter what. The couple can stop intercourse or stop stimulating each other and her orgasm will happen regardless.

SEXUAL RESPONSE CYCLE
ORGASM IN WOMEN

The female orgasm phase is characterized by involuntary muscle contractions, which entails the vagina/orgasmic platform/outer third of the vagina swelling and tightening, the uterus contracting (similar to labor), and muscles in other parts of the body, like the feet, contracting. The woman's body is flooded with endorphins, which provide feelings of happiness and elation. Oxytocin is also released, which bonds the couple.

It is important to note that most women require direct clitoral stimulation for orgasm. The intensity of the woman's orgasm varies from woman to woman and from orgasm to orgasm. Women are capable of having multiple orgasms during each sexual encounter while men are not. They do not have the presence of what is called a refractory period, which is a time frame needed prior to another orgasm. Typically, the refractory period will only allow for a man to have one orgasm per sexual encounter.

SEXUAL RESPONSE CYCLE
RESOLUTION IN WOMEN

The female resolution phase is where blood vessels dilate to drain the pelvic region; there is a loss of muscle tension (sense of increased relaxation); the vagina returns to normal; the uterus drops back to the normal position; and the cervix opens and drops into the seminal pool (for twenty to thirty minutes after the orgasm). The process of the cervix dropping into the seminal pool is for the purpose of insemination. Many women want to cuddle or talk with their partner, as they feel very close and connected by the process.

SEXUAL RESPONSE CYCLE
DESIRE IN MEN

The male desire phase is more characterized by thoughts or visual stimuli than by the relationship quality. Research shows us that significantly more men than women have desire for sex when there is just sexual stimulation alone. There are plenty of men who desire intercourse due to relationship satisfaction, however. Some men may experience an increase in sexual desire with an increase in the stress response. This can be due in part to sexual programming in youth. Men who have masturbated to decrease stress are conditioned to respond with sexual desire when their stress levels increase. Men are typically more aware of their sexual desire than women, especially in a conservative society where women are wrongly taught, explicitly or not, that sexual desire is wrong. Men are more likely to move from desire to arousal than women.

SEXUAL RESPONSE CYCLE AROUSAL/EXCITEMENT IN MEN

The male arousal/excitement phase, like the female phase, includes vaso-congestion. This blood engorges the penis and produces an erection. This is the key indicator for men that they are in the arousal phase of the SRC. The man's scrotum thickens, and the spermatic cord shortens. The Cowper's gland secretes fluid. This is what some term precum. This fluid prepares the urethra for the male ejaculate, which occurs with orgasm; insemination can happen with this fluid. Women don't require this because their urethra only produces urine and isn't the avenue for an ejaculate like it is for men. Men are capable of moving from desire to arousal in a few seconds.

SEXUAL RESPONSE CYCLE PLATEAU IN MEN

The male plateau phase is also called the foreplay or love play stage. In this stage, the testes increase in size by as much as 50 percent. Semen, which is a collection of fluids from the testes, seminal vesicle, Cowper's gland, and prostate, has collected at the base of the penis internally in different structures, awaiting orgasm for release. Many people think that sperm are produced in the testicles and wait there for orgasm. This is not the case. There is a lot more to this life-giving process. The Cowper's gland secretes a pre-ejaculate that prepares the urethra for the semen. The pre-ejaculate neutralizes the acid that urine has left in the urethra and lubricates the urethra to limit mechanical damage during ejaculation. This stage can last from five to forty-five minutes. The plateau phase ends with the "moment of ejaculatory inevitability," when ejaculation will happen no matter what. This is similar to the female "moment of orgasmic inevitability." It is highly important to note that no damage is done to the man if he doesn't ejaculate. It can be uncomfortable, but despite what many men believe, there is no damage incurred.

SEXUAL RESPONSE CYCLE
ORGASM IN MEN

The male orgasmic phase includes contractions that force semen and ejaculate to be released from their respective internal structures and to be expelled through the urethra. Internal contractions occur with the vas deferens, seminal vesicles, and prostate gland. Other muscle tightening, such as in the legs or feet, is normal during this phase. The size of the penis decreases fairly immediately, and there is general relaxation and a release of dopamine, oxytocin, and other endorphins. Dopamine makes the man feel pleasure and elation.

SEXUAL RESPONSE CYCLE
RESOLUTION IN MEN

In the male resolution phase, blood leaves the pelvic area, the penis returns to its unaroused size, the testes descend, and there is a refractory period. A refractory period is a period of time during which the man can't have another orgasm; it can last from five minutes to twenty-four hours, depending on the man and his age.

I have worked with countless couples who are frustrated at how quickly the man goes from desire to orgasm. Upon investigation, these men do not struggle with what we would call premature ejaculation but rather simply do not need the same time that it takes for their wives to go through the sexual response cycle. This is normal for most couples. If you are like these many couples, you will need to learn a better cadence of pace throughout the entire sexual encounter. If you were having sex alone, there wouldn't be an issue. However, you are not alone and likely desperately want your partner to be as satisfied as you are. As a companion, you will need to learn some techniques that will enable you to be sexually and emotionally present without racing through to the climactic finish line. You will find many of these techniques throughout this book. The chapter Common Questions & Solutions provides such an illustration.

Ben, a former client, learned some of these techniques during treatment. He learned that the mere presence of an erection didn't mean that intercourse should shortly ensue, but rather that gently and lovingly waiting for his wife's arousal to build was a better course. Gabriela would then signal a more appropriate time for intercourse. He also learned that quickly thrusting to maximize pleasure would only leave him partially satisfied, since Gabriela would be left wanting, and he would be left feeling disappointed in himself. Ben slowed down intercourse and included elements of soft thrusting and deep penetration with accompanying pelvic rotation and rubbing his pelvis against his wife's clitoris. He also found that pacing intercourse with his wife made climax more satisfying and found greater sexual competence and control. Ben and Gabriela enjoyed more opportunities to orgasm together as well, which increased their bond one to another.

I want to talk for a moment about personal lubricant. As discussed earlier in the manuscript, women have significant vaginal lubricant during stages with arousal. Because people are all different, some women produce more or less vaginal lubricant than others. Life stage and contextual factors can also play a role in vaginal lubrication. For instance, when women go through menopause, vaginal lubricant significantly decreases. In other cases, vaginal lubricant is not sufficient during the moments when penetration occurs or, at times, not at all during a particular sexual experience. In these instances, I encourage the couple to obtain personal lubricant that is water based for sexual intercourse. Oil-based lubricants or lubricants that heat, cool, or tingle are sometimes associated with discomfort or pain. Water-based lubricants can be purchased at almost any grocery store by the condom section. I want to make something clear: most couples can benefit from the use of personal lubricant in their sexual relationships.

ᔥ *ACTIVITY* ᖾ

This section's activity builds on the last chapter's activity. As you remember, we just left off with each partner having a great awareness of his or her uniquely and magnificently designed sexual anatomy. Each partner should have had the opportunity to find what touch, intensity, and placement of touch feels pleasurable and how to increase this pleasure. You were then directed to show your spouse by him or her first watching you illustrate this touch and then participating in it.

The next progressive step is for the spouse to try and replicate what he or she has been taught. In keeping with the last section's activity, I will speak as if the wife is teaching her husband the touch she desires. The husband is now going solo and is to use his hand and try to replicate what the wife has been teaching him without any form of shadowing. He is to be responsive to verbal correction. Husbands, keep in mind that your wife is not being critical of you. You are not a bad husband for not knowing how to do this. It is simply irrational to think that you would be good at this; you are not her and cannot be in her head. Even if you have had sexual encounters before marriage, your wife is an individual and has her own sexual appetite, has her own likes and dislikes, and is in large part still exploring what these are. Wives, give your husband a break; as long as he is learning and understanding your sexual needs, encourage him.

A word of caution: it is likely that as the husband becomes aroused by the sexual encounter, he will begin doing sexual touch that he thinks will feel good to his wife based on his sexual appetite, experience, understanding of women, likes, and dislikes. This most likely will vary from what his wife really needs. I strongly advise against this. It will defeat the purpose of the activity. The activity is to learn about your spouse. Allow her preferences to be your guide. You may have to re-wire sexual scripts you have learned throughout life in media and society.

The next step is to transition from manual stimulation to intercourse. The couple should begin with the manual stimulation that has been taught to the husband. A mix of manual stimulation, caressing touch, and other forms of foreplay are encouraged before intercourse. Sex is a very interactive process. Do not wait around for the husband's erection to occur or for the wife to start becoming aroused in order to begin foreplay. Be engaged and active. In most instances, when you focus on touch and interaction that is all about sexual and sensual pleasure, sufficient lubrication and erection will follow. Keep in mind that women usually desire and need more foreplay than men prior to intercourse. This will most likely be substantially more time than the husband might think requisite. When you are both sufficiently aroused and ready for intercourse, the wife is to signal to her husband. When seeking intercourse from a foreplay encounter, only pursue when your hope is to increase pleasure. Do not pursue it as the means to an end or as the goal. If intercourse seems like it would feel good, then move to that.

Additionally, I would like you to think of the various SRCs and how they relate to your sexual experiences. Is there a model that fits you more than the rest? Is your experience something altogether different? After taking a few moments to think about this, talk to your partner about your SRC. Women, if you identify with the Basson model, talk to your partner about the conscious choices you make to move from desire to arousal. Discuss what sex is like when this decision is left out. Men, tell your partner how you feel about seeing your SRC in a more nonlinear light. It may be difficult to imagine embracing your erection ebbing and flowing, since society has wrongly taught you that men don't lose an erection during intercourse. To go above and beyond in this section, you can look up clips at covenantsextherapy.com/book that show what happens internally for the production of semen and all of the elements included in seminal fluid. You can also see the changes in the vaginal barrel, uterus, and cervix through the SRC.

In the space below, write down what you are learning about your spouse. What was it like for you to be the one providing manual touch for their pleasure? What challenges did you find? What successes did you have? Where are you going to go from here? Maybe there is room for improvement and you two have some direction that you would like to follow over the next week or so. Write these thoughts down.

*What do you need to be **attentive** to from this chapter?*

_____

_____

*What do you need to be **accountable** for from this chapter?*

_____

_____

*What do you need to **accept** about this chapter?*

_____

_____

*What needs to be **re-storied** from this chapter?*

_____

_____

GENDER DIFFERENCES

*I*t is truly a great thing that men and women are different. It appears at first glance that exact similarity would bring about more sexual satisfaction in the couple's relationship. However, I think that this idea doesn't hold up as well when examined a little more closely. The variety and augmentation that are provided when combining two individuals' unique sexualities have the potential to be exponentially greater than if there were no dissimilarity. This still doesn't mean that it's any easier wading through sexual differences. Some of the roadblocks that come with these differences include sexual desire/frequency, fantasy, foreplay, pleasure, and sexual positions. This section will cover the main differences, or roadblocks, that I have found anecdotally and have researched, as well as interventions or activities typically prescribed in the field of sex therapy.

One of the pitfalls that most couples allow to be present is that of their sexual differences. Instead of enthusiastically embracing their sexual differences and creating a brand-new sexual culture between the couple, they usually get stuck trying to bring their spouse over to their side. When both partners are trying to do this, they don't get very far. What they get is an unhealthy negative cycle of interaction surrounding sexuality that is anything but satisfying, not to mention being the farthest thing from sexually arousing and pleasuring. It's no wonder why most of these couples have at least one partner who struggles with low sexual desire. In their book on sexual wholeness, Busby, Carroll, and Leavitt attempt to get couples to embrace these differences as a way to augment their sexual relationships.[1] They describe the partner who experiences quicker arousal and desire for sexual intimacy as one who helps prioritize sex in the relationship and the partner with slower arousal and desire as the one who helps the couple appreciate the journey of sexual intimacy. When men and women stop trying to get their partners to be exactly like them, they stand to gain the most out of their sexual relationships. This type of sexual teamwork is the best approach to having transcendent sexual intimacy.

Men usually want to have sex *to feel* emotionally close and connected, while women want to have sex *when they feel* emotionally close and connected. I have seen that when couples take this to heart, there is an extremely transformative process that takes place in their sexual relationships. As a healthy side effect, their marital satisfaction also increases. Research shows a strong correlation between marital satisfaction and sexual satisfaction. My doctoral chair would say that "for women, sex starts in the kitchen." This has been something quoted for years, but it highlights a difference in the reasons men and women engage in sexual intercourse.

The idea is that women need to feel loved, cared for, special, important, valued, and thought of as more than a sexual object or outlet. Some of the ways that women feel this are through their partners helping out around the house, taking care of the kids, asking about their busy day, listening to them, dating, or speaking kind words to them or about them. This is especially important considering that the SRC for women entails a decision to allow sexual desire and arousal. It is difficult for women to choose to feel sexual desire and arousal when they don't feel special, loved, cared for, or connected to their spouses. Without such, it is difficult for women to engage in a satisfying sexual encounter. Moreover, without feeling close prior to sex, women have a difficult time performing sexually. Being sufficiently lubricated and having an orgasm becomes significantly more difficult. When his partner doesn't feel close and connected, it makes it ever more difficult for the husband to build off of his partner's sexual arousal, limiting the satisfaction for both partners. Therefore, it is just as crucial for a woman to receive emotional foreplay as it is for a man to receive physical foreplay.

For those who do not take this seriously, try simple physical foreplay for your wife before sex and you will see what I mean. It's just like the wife not providing the physical stimulation—touching, kissing, et cetera—that produces an erection for the man. It makes intercourse impossible or unenjoyable. Without the wife feeling loved, cared for, special, or bonded, it makes intercourse unenjoyable or, at times, impossible.

When the woman feels connected and cared for by her spouse and chooses to allow sexual desire and arousal in, there are some interesting changes. She will be more aroused by sexual touch. Women report that clitoral, labial, breast, and nipple stimulation are arousing when emotional foreplay takes place. Prior to emotional foreplay, their clitorises, labium, breasts, and nipples don't feel much of anything when they are touched by their spouses, and women are at times irritated by such touch or feel "groped" by their spouses. When emotion and body are in unison, the woman's arousal is likely to build. Therefore, the emotional connection and body are equally valuable arousal components in women. When these are not intertwined, the woman often struggles sexually.

Historically, men don't struggle as much with desire, arousal, and orgasm as women do because they have lower thresholds for arousal and orgasm, as stated by Busby, Carroll, and Leavitt.[2] Culture plays a big part of why this is so. Even within our highly conservative culture, there are messages that portray men as positive sexual beings. It isn't uncommon in our culture to hear such things as "He shouldn't have done that, but boys will be boys," or "Guys are always thinking about sex." Similar messages for women don't exist. Messages like "She's highly sexual" (in a negative tone) or "Good girls don't think about stuff like that" are predominant for women, thus suppressing their sexuality. If women were taught to honor their sexual desire and arousal all through their lives and to think of themselves as sexual beings, while still following their religious values of abstinence, they most likely wouldn't have higher arousal and orgasm thresholds. At the very least, this wouldn't be a contributing factor.

There is one caveat to the aforementioned point, and it relates to Basson's model of the sexual response cycle. Because emotional foreplay is more vital for women than men, it is important to highlight the decision factor—namely, whether or not she wants or is open to allowing a sexual flow from desire to orgasm. In essence, as Basson described, women make a decision to allow in desire and arousal.

A while back I had a couple who fit right into this mold. Malik was extremely frustrated because he would provide Jasmine adequate clitoral stimulation and related touch before and during intercourse. However,

Jasmine would still not become sexually aroused for sufficient lubrication or orgasm or to enjoy the sexual experience. With time, Jasmine began discussing her feelings of emotional disconnectedness and criticism that made her feel less bonded and cared for in the overall relationship. After working on these attachment injuries, Jasmine began enjoying her sexual relationship, and her body physiologically followed in kind.

As therapists say, "Sometimes we learn more from our clients than they do from us." A few years back, a teaching moment for one of the couples I met with turned into a teaching moment for me. I discussed some of the reasons why men and women engage in sex, as partially described above. The next session the wife referenced my psychological education and said, "It really helped me to hear that my husband feels loved, important, and even invincible when we have sex. Knowing how it impacts him has really helped me to want to try harder to improve our sex life and take charge of my sexuality, as well as letting go of some of the resentment I was holding." Until that moment I had really tried hard to not send the message that women need to have sex with their husbands because it's important for the husbands to feel loved. I did this because I didn't want wives to feel that it was their duty. However, this interchange caused me to reevaluate this concern.

I noticed that I'd been blind to the fact that the husband had some valid concerns and that sex was very important for feeling loved. While I did not want to perpetuate the idea of "duty," this precaution neglected the fact that one way of feeling loved is not better than another. I guess it was a subconscious way of realigning equality between the sexes. The more I reflected on this, the more I realized the immense importance for the wife to have sex with her husband as a way for him to feel loved. This *is* a duty, just as it is *his* duty to verbally express love or for him to protect her or nurture the relationship. It should not be a duty that wives or husbands do begrudgingly but out of gratitude for this holy right.

I want to highlight that this should not be the sole way for him to receive love and that the wife should not have sex whenever the husband wants, but the wife should make it a point to show her love by engaging in sex regularly and with excitement and enthusiasm, just as the husband should. I thank that client for the teaching moment she gave me. We owe it to our partners to partake of the whole experience of marriage. We should not be picking and choosing what aspects of marriage we want to engage in, especially in covenant marriages. We engage in all aspects, or else we are not striving for a godly marriage. Busby, Carrol, and Leavitt contend that sex is a vital part of salvation and principle to God's plan.

Now I would like to talk about varying types of desire. This covers men and women and through different stages of life and relationship. The stereotypical desire needs no introduction. Society portrays this with the idea that a man or woman wants to be intimate because he or she craves for physical touch and caressing with his or her partner. While there is nothing wrong with this, I want to mention alternate types of sexual desire that are equally effective and important. Different reasons you or your partner might have for sex include a desire to be with one's partner to build emotional closeness, a desire to show closeness felt, a desire to sexually fulfill your partner, a desire to relieve stress, or an enjoyment this type of varying time spent with your partner. There is nothing wrong with this. Embrace these different drives to be intimate, and hopefully your spouse will as well. Your spouse, or even you, may question the fact that you don't desire sex solely because it feels good. This is normal to feel, but it's not accurate. You should never see yourself as less sexual or as someone who doesn't enjoy sex just because you aren't craving sex because of physiological reasons (though you may really enjoy the physiological payoff afterward).

FANTASY

Much of our understanding concerning men and women and sexual fantasy is that men fantasize and think about sex more often than women do. My education and experience has shown me that this is not always the case. However, I will speak to the majority of both men and women. Fantasies and time spent contemplating sex does something unique for men. It programs them to be more sexual, to crave sex, and to stay in the moment during a sexual encounter. Women often struggle calming the thoughts in their minds to focus on sexuality. Even in a restful state, the minds of women are substantially more active than for men.[4] Men typically stoke the fire and keep it simmering so that the slightest interest from their spouse can turn into a flame in the matter of seconds. When do they do this? Well in their mental down time of course. Women spend little time stoking the sexual fire and because of this need to spend more time getting kindling, matches, or drying out the firewood. Why don't women stoke the fire? They have little mental down time.

If you were to think about chocolate, fantasize about how it tastes, how it melts in your mouth, and how it feels as you bite down on an expensive bar of it, and if you spend a great deal of your day in these thoughts and in this preoccupation, you might gain some insight into the stereotypical man's world. How difficult would it be for you to avoid buying or consuming a bar of chocolate after a week spent in this fantasy and consumption of thought? I might assume that you in this very moment now crave chocolate quite a bit more than when reading the previous paragraph. Now think of years—no, decades—of thinking this much about chocolate, maybe twenty times a day, being overtaken by these thoughts. You may only now be gaining some insight into the reasons why men are generally more desirous of sexual encounters than women.

Should a woman want to increase her sexual desire, I would propose programming herself differently than in all her years prior. Try thinking about sex, being touched, having an orgasm, and fantasizing about your spouse several times a day for weeks on end. I would be shocked if you didn't report a higher sexual desire at week four than at day one.

With many women in therapy struggling with the issues of low sexual desire, I'd like to provide an example of the above mentioned. Samantha and Ezra told the all-too-familiar story of Samantha's limited desire for sex. Ezra felt that he did all the right things before and during sex to arouse his wife, but to no avail. Samantha had tried some things told to her by friends and family whom she had confided in, but these similarly didn't bring the desired outcome. I sat across this desperate couple anxious to give them some counsel that could change their lives. It all depended on whether they would implement and with what mentality they would follow through.

I started off by turning to Ezra and asking him to describe how often he thought of sex in a week, fantasized about his wife, or hoped that they would be intimate. He gave me the sought-after reply. "Weekly? I think about sex several times a day." He took the bait.

I asked Samantha the same question. She couldn't have replied any better. "Maybe a few times a month," she said. I went on to tell them both that Ezra nurtures his sexual desire on a daily basis. It has become second nature, but he unwittingly spends a significant amount of his time fostering sexuality. Therefore, he is regularly interested in a sexual encounter. I then explained that Samantha's lack of nurturing produces what one might imagine, leaving her with limited to no sexual desire. Samantha was given the charge to find out what nurturing sexual desire on a daily basis looks like for her and to begin implementing it.

This can go the other way as well. If a man spends a substantial amount of time thinking about sex and stoking the fire then he's going to want to have sex more and be less available for other forms of connection. Thus, men typically need to put work into finding other forms of connection and engagement with their spouse so that the partner feels like more than a sexual object. I think this is why more men struggle with pornography and masturbation than women. They spend a lot of time in a sexualizing state of mind.

FOREPLAY

Another gender pitfall I see in therapy is that couples do not engage in enough foreplay for the wife to be aroused sufficiently for intercourse to be pleasurable or, at times, even possible. The old adage that men are like a microwave and women are like an oven in terms of sexual arousal is true for many couples. In a life where you have many obligations and children who only sleep a few hours through the night, you may fall victim to the idea of rushing through to intercourse. Please don't fall victim to this. Make an extra fifteen to twenty minutes available for your wife to build sexual arousal. It's only fair, not to mention that her arousal is going to make your experience a thousand times more pleasurable. If you neglect this, her body will not be ready and primed for intercourse. She may experience discomfort and low satisfaction. It's the equivalent of her saying, "Insert your penis while it's only partially erect." That wouldn't be pleasurable or even possible at times.

A recent couple in counseling with limited sexual satisfaction learned the importance of this principle. Lauren often complained that she didn't enjoy sex as much as she had hoped or as much as she had in the past. Seth was willing to make any needed changes, but the couple was at the end of their rope and had tried all that they could fathom. Over several months, Seth and Lauren began applying some principles taught in therapy that made all the difference. They had a relatively good sexual relationship. There were some minor changes that needed to be made, which made all the difference. One of these was that Seth would initiate intercourse before Lauren was appropriately aroused. Seth's arousal built quicker than Lauren's, and he would move to sex when he was ready. Lauren didn't think much of this and would accept his advances when he felt ready. Part of Lauren's issue was derived from society's implicit messages to women that their sexuality isn't as important as men's sexuality. Lauren learned to honor her sexuality by way of giving time for her arousal to build. Seth learned that transitioning to intercourse when he was ready and Lauren was still building arousal was the same as Lauren transitioning to intercourse when Seth only had a partial erection. They both could see that it was counterproductive to move to sex when Lauren was still building arousal. The couple found great joy in both partners being ready for intercourse and found that a much more fulfilling sex life followed.

What leads to this type of interaction is when sex occurs only at night after you and your spouse are both exhausted. This type of routine sex doesn't make it easy for you or your spouse to take the extra time to build the woman's arousal, not to mention that routine sex of this nature kills sexual desire. You should be having sex at different times of the day and in different settings if possible. It's an important part of your relationship and should be made a priority.

SEXUAL ANATOMY & SEXUAL UNDERSTANDING

One of my favorite topics to teach in sex therapy is that of gender differences in self-sexual education or the way in which boys and girls teach themselves about their bodies. As discussed, the male and female anatomies are similar, but there are a few ways in which they differ. These differences are quite significant. The one that I want to discuss briefly is that of the external male anatomy versus the internal female anatomy structure. As boys grow and develop, they are much aware of their penises and testicles, the two major parts of their sexual anatomy system. One way that men learn about their sexual anatomy is through daily contact.

All men touch their penis several times on a daily basis. Let me clarify. To urinate, a man has to touch his penis. Similarly, there is adjusting of the penis that takes place. This increases comfort, awareness, and confidence for the man with his penis. Whether attempting to or not, a male will have contact with his penis when he is experiencing a partial or full erection. For example, it may be that while urinating he happens to have a partial erection. Touching his penis to urinate will provide some form of stimulation by the sheer fact that there are nerve endings all over his penis that he is touching to hold his penis. This process is just one way in which he learns that certain touches provide erectile capability and pleasure. While he is not necessarily trying to arouse himself, this daily touch enables him to sense what is more or less sexually arousing, where he is more sensitive, and how his penis feels when it becomes aroused through this touch. Similarly, he can see that he has the crucial parts necessary to be sexually intimate. Men can see if their penis is engorged with blood and an erection takes place, full or partial. Not only do they see this process occur, but they see every step of the way, thus making it a lot easier to track their sexual arousal and have confidence in the process occurring and in their ability to build arousal when they are married and sexual encounters take place.

During urination is not the only time that men learn about their sexual anatomy. While changing, showering, and going about their day, men are learning. They are able to feel their penis becoming erect as it makes contact with their thigh or their clothing. They can teach themselves how to get an erection to dissipate or increase in arousal through their mental engagement and varying types of contact or movement against their clothing, their body, or their hand. All four of these awarenesses—physiological, mental, visual, and tactile—dramatically increase a man's knowledge and confidence in his sexual performance. So, when he is married, he is very well trained and educated as to his own body and can engage in a sexual encounter with more confidence.

I believe that the inherent external genitalia do two other things that sometimes complicate matters. First, men are more erotically focused and preoccupied than women in general. With all the touching, adjusting, and movement to the penis, men are even more prone to think of sex and even act on sexual arousal alone, with pornography or another person. This then contributes to the rise in our culture of unwanted sexual behavior or even compulsive/addictive sexual behavior being more prominent with men than with women. Second, the increased awareness of the penis, those things arousing, the penis's movement or touch with clothing/chair, etc., and any slight change in blood flow set the resting brain of a man in an eroticized state. This can become an issue as constant petitions for sex or over focus on sexuality pull at the overall relationship satisfaction.

Due to the internal nature of the female sexual anatomy, women have things a little more difficult. Women do not have unavoidable educational contact with the main center of sexual arousal, their clitorises. There is not a daily routine, such as urination, that forces them to have contact with their clitorises. When urination does occur, the touch they engage in entails the use of a piece of toilet paper. So the limited contact they have with their sexual anatomy, the vulva, is dulled. For visual clitoral contact to take place, the woman would need to seek this out. Many women in our culture would not feel comfortable in doing so without being taught that this is all right or a normal curiosity. Such teaching is scarce. Additionally, when arousal does occur, the smaller size of the exposed portion of the clitoris and concealed/protected nature of the clitoris makes it difficult for the woman to be as aware of this and how to increase or decrease this arousal, which men more easily learn.

I want to highlight that a woman may have just as much if not more arousal than some men. However, lubrication and clitoral engorgement or erection is just much more difficult to feel or become aware of than a man's erection. Thus, a lot of women are not aware of having any arousal, what it looks like when they are aroused, what it feels like, and how to increase or decrease it. Furthermore, LDS culture typically discourages education of, awareness of, and tracking of arousal for fear that it might lead to sexually acting out or inappropriate responding. Additionally, men are more prone to have sexual desire with touch or physiological arousal alone over women.

HOW WOMEN HAVE SEX

A crucial difference in men and women is that of sexual positions and associated techniques for optimal sexual performance and satisfaction. Most couples are not aware that this is something they need to work on. Most often, the woman just chalks up her dissatisfaction with intercourse to sex not being something that is for women or for her. The fact of the matter is that the way most couples have sex is actually not for women.

Most couples have sex in such a way that the type of penetration and associated movement is geared toward men. Don't get too frustrated with yourselves; the larger society as a whole incorrectly teaches us this. The husband, while he enjoys their typical sexual position and movement, is not entirely satisfied either. He is able to have an orgasm but finds a lack of complete satisfaction since his wife is not fulfilled. The couple may feel at times that sex is just for the man and that the wife is just there because she has to be in order for sex to take place, thus making sex feel more like an individualistic act. He imagines that if she were sexually satisfied, he would find much more satisfaction with intercourse as well. You see, the typical, quick, in-and-out thrusting of the penis into the vaginal canal feels good . . . for men. It *usually* doesn't feel pleasurable for women. You see, there aren't many nerve endings in the vaginal canal. Below I will provide a position and associated technique that will be satisfying for women and men.

For brevity's sake, I want to introduce the more-referenced position for increasing clitoral stimulation, without manual stimulation, during intercourse. This position is called the coital alignment technique (CAT) (Eichel & Nobile, 1992). The CAT is a position that produces a significant amount of direct clitoral stimulation during intercourse. With this position, clitoral stimulation is constant and has associated movement that gives a more generalized rubbing feel to the clitoris and connected region.

In the CAT, the man is lying on top of the woman (the modified CAT has the woman on the top). He inserts his penis entirely into the vaginal canal. This is the position in which the penis stays during this sexual technique. There is no in-and-out moving or thrusting. The man is to rotate and thrust his hips so that the base of the penis and pelvis are pushing against the woman's clitoris and vulva. It is this point of contact, the base of the penis and the man's pelvis against the woman's clitoris, from which pleasure is derived for the woman. She is to similarly rotate and thrust her pelvis, which exposes and pushes the clitoris against the base of the penis and the man's pelvis. The movement is more of a rubbing and up-and-down thrusting where contact is constant. The wife may find that she is lifting her hips up, possibly off the bed, and rotating/thrusting her hips toward her stomach.

The basic idea to have in mind is that the clitoris needs constant rubbing from the man's genitalia or pelvis in order for her to find pleasure or orgasm during intercourse. Any other technique or position that is going to provide stimulation to the woman's clitoris is going to include the man having his penis inserted deeply, which enables the clitoris to make contact with the base of the penis and pelvis, and movement or thrusting will consist of a slow, more grinding movement, which may increase with pace as her arousal increases and orgasm occurs. Other positions in which the husband or wife provides manual clitoral stimulation during intercourse are also highly effective. Such positions include man sitting on the edge of the bed or chair with the woman sitting on top either chest to chest or facing away. When facing chest to chest the woman can stimulate the clitoris. When facing away either partner can stimulate the clitoris. Another position that lends itself to the woman stimulating her clitoris includes the woman kneeling on the bed with her head resting on a pillow. The man enters from behind also kneeling. The woman can stimulate her clitoris during penetration.

It was the third session in therapy, and Sara and Jeff could hardly contain themselves. They almost burst into my office door and shouted the good news. "Sara had three orgasms over the last week," Jeff said with a smile he could hardly contain. Sara repeatedly nodded with a similarly enthusiastic smile. The couple had struggled over the last several years of marriage to bring Sara to climax. Every so often she was able to have an orgasm, but at times it would go a year or more between successes. Sara described how much more sensation and pleasure she felt while they explored the new technique that was taught to them at the last therapy session.

The CAT was prescribed as a means for Sara to feel more sensation during intercourse. The couple was assigned to go home and play around with this new technique. They were cautioned to not get too hung up on the exact motion of the CAT, but rather to apply the basic principle of clitoral stimulation through rubbing against Jeff's pelvis and the base of his penis. This adaptive couple didn't struggle with creatively modifying the technique to a rocking motion that was more appealing to them. Jeff was excited not only to have a technique that Sara really enjoyed but also to have a technique that made it easier for him to refrain from climaxing before Sara's pleasure built. The modification to a non-in-and-out thrusting enabled him to enjoy a firm erection without climaxing significantly sooner than before. Sara and Jeff are a great example of how an adaptive couple can, with a little psychological education, turn a low-satisfaction sex life into a vibrant one.

ACTIVITY

With all this in mind, it is vital that women be more purposeful concerning their sexual learning about themselves. Typically, the diagnosis of anorgasmia, the inability to have an orgasm, is given to women, with far fewer men reporting this issue. This activity and encouragement is that a couple reading this should start tracking their sexual desire and arousal as well as reasons for desire and arousal. This will take some work, as men will have a lot to report and women will need to put a great deal of effort into increasing awareness. Men, just get writing. Women, there are several ways to begin.

Women can periodically stop their busy lives and literally examine what is going on for them sexually and physiologically. We all have arousal throughout the day. However, many women have trained themselves not to be aware of this. I implore you to start training and programming yourself to become aware of your sexual arousal. Spend a few moments by yourself thinking about your sexual organs. Is there more sensitivity to your vulva or clitoris? Do certain movements or focus on arousal increase or decrease pleasure and arousal? Does touch to your clitoris, vulva, or vaginal canal bring out further arousal? Do you have more lubrication or less than when you checked earlier in the day? Has the vaginal canal changed its form or tightness (check with your finger if comfortable)? Write it down in the space below:

After you have done your writing, share this with your spouse. Try to find ways to augment what you already have by way of desire and arousal to be a more complete partner. Finally, put this into action. Talk to your spouse throughout the day when desire and arousal occur. Send your spouse a flirty text or drop by the office or the house on a quick break to tell him or her how aroused you have been or what aroused you.

*What do you need to be **attentive** to from this chapter?*

_____

_____

*What do you need to be **accountable** for from this chapter?*

_____

_____

*What do you need to **accept** about this chapter?*

_____

_____

*What needs to be **re-storied** from this chapter?*

_____

_____

✣ NOTES ✣

1. See Dean M. Busby, Jason S. Carroll, and Chelom Leavitt, *Sexual Wholeness in Marriage: An LDS Perspective on Integrating Sexuality and Spirituality in Our Marriages* (United States of America: Book Printers of Utah, 2013).
2. See Busby, Carroll, and Leavitt.
3. Busby, Carroll, and Leavitt, 38.
4. Daniel G. Amen, *Sex on the Brain: 12 Lessons to Enhance Your Love Life* (New York: Three Rivers Press, 2008), 81.

SEXUAL ADDICTION
& the SEXUAL
RELATIONSHIP

*A*bout two-thirds of my clients have some sort of sexual dysfunction or issue of satisfaction. Roughly the other third have a sexual addiction. Most often these sexual addiction clients struggle with pornography and masturbation. Men are my typical clients of this type; however, women also come to therapy with these same issues. This chapter isn't about overcoming addiction. There are many great books on that subject. I have included references to these books at my website, covenantsextherapy.com/resources. This chapter is on how sexual addiction impacts sexual relationships and what can be done by the former or current addict and the spouse to improve couple intimacy. While I believe that an entire book can be written on the impact of sexual addiction on sexual relationships and the best practices of couples who have struggled or do struggle with addiction, I will follow my initial objective of brevity and only hit the highlight points. Sexual compulsivity or addictions cause five typical sexual issues in the addict or spouse. They are connection, spirituality, mutual satisfaction, safety and vulnerability, and performance.

CONNECTION

Connection is at the heart of any healthy sexual relationship. When sex is void of connection, a couple really struggles. Research has shown that women are more driven by connection that leads to sexual desire than erotic or sexual touch alone. A partner of an addict may experience sexual dysfunction such as low sexual desire or anorgasmia as a result of the addiction. An example of how this may form might be that the partner of the addict may be too preoccupied with fears that his or her partner is thinking of pornography to enjoy the sexual encounter, therefore emotionally and cognitively removing the spouse from the sexual encounter. Once emotionally and cognitively removed, sexual performance is restricted. The partner may not long for sex or could have a very difficult time reaching an orgasm. Research has also shown us that pertinent sexual programming software is uploaded into all of us as we experience early or prevalent sexual experiences. When pornography and masturbation are such early or prevalent sexual experiences, our brain begins to wire sexuality and expression with disconnection instead of connection. As the addict amasses copious amounts of time with engaging this brain wiring, the individual distances further and further from the inherent wiring that God had hoped for us, namely wiring sexuality and expression with connection.

The couple needs to learn how to reconnect during sexual intimacy. The addict must learn how to re-wire or re-program their sexuality with connection. Being aware of how selfishness comes into the sexual relationship, making and accepting petitions for connection, and learning to be emotionally and cognitively present with one's spouse will be the gateway to a healthy connected sexual relationship.

Write down some of the ways you have identified disconnection and how you have felt connection or might feel connection:

_____

_____

_____

_____

_____

_____

_____

_____

BRINGING SPIRITUALITY
INTO THE BEDROOM

Spirituality has long been a dimension of the sexual relationship that our LDS culture has valued. However, many get perplexed as to what this looks like in the sexual relationship. Referring to sexuality in marriage, Jeffery R. Holland says it's "a symbol of total union: union of their hearts, their hopes, their lives, their love, their family, their future, their everything."[1] The easiest way for me to explain this to my clients is that when spirituality is brought into the couple's sex life, sexual expression becomes more than the physical, emotional, or connection. Sexual expression becomes an exclamation point to the "togetherness" of the couple. It is the exclamation point to the couple's togetherness of hearts, hopes, lives, love, family, future, everything. Therefore, when the couple is sexual they feel that "togetherness" in manifestation of sexual expression.

Couples where one or both partners struggle with pornography become distanced from the spirit and have a difficult time feeling that spiritual togetherness inside and outside of the bedroom. This may also be the case where pornography is a thing of the past. Many couples find themselves in recovery, but still lack that spiritual element in their sex lives. Often pornography prevented the couple from experiencing the spiritual oneness from existing in the couple's sex lives and they haven't a clue how to bring what never was into the bedroom with them.

I have found that when this is the case, the couple needs to align their hearts, hopes, lives, love, family, future—everything more. They often find that by doing so, their sex life alters. If this doesn't produce the desired results, the couple can work on the first element of connection during sex and the fourth element, safety and vulnerability. As they make these changes they will find that sex goes from being strictly physical to comprising other elements of connecting, emotional, relaxing, and exclamatory of their togetherness.

EFFECTS OF PORNOGRAPHY ON SEX

The research on pornography shows us that it produces some pretty staggering results in terms of sexual satisfaction. These results undoubtedly impact the mutual satisfaction of the couple and performance. Decreased sexual satisfaction as a couple can lead to diminished sexual activity, relationship decline, and a host of other sexual struggles. It is not uncommon to have an addict or recovered addict limited in their satisfaction with their partner's performance, body, affection, and so on. Sexual scripting theory posits that cultural scenarios, interpersonal scripts, and intrapsychic scripts are applied to sexual behavior.[2] In layman's terms, what is seen in pornography becomes part of the sexual scripts that people develop for sex, expression, men, and women. We desire and act out of these scripts. As these scripts play out or do not play out in the sexual relationship, an addict or former addict can become increasingly dissatisfied. The hyper-focus on these scripts detracts from the partner's satisfaction with sex. Mutual satisfaction becomes a common complaint of these couples.

Re-scripting must then take place. Essentially the addict or former addict goes from a sexual script, including such things as one person being in control, male-centric sexuality, distorted image of bodies, or sexuality lacking a humanistic side to a script including things such as partner engagement, responsive sexuality, connection, getting outside of oneself, and a varied view of sexual expression. In the space below, please write down your sexual scripts and what has contributed to these scripts. Then indicate healthy script changes for you and your spouse and experiences that will foster these:

_____

_____

_____

_____

_____

_____

_____

SAFETY & VULNERABILITY

Safety and vulnerability are important elements for a successful sexual relationship. However, when there has been a sexual addiction, safety and vulnerability are *essential* for a healthy sexual relationship. Do not mistake the fact that you and your spouse are having sex of any kind for having healthy and healing sex. The traumatized partner may be grasping for ways to keep you entertained in the relationship and feel that allowing you to have sex whenever you want will keep you faithful and free from acting out with yourself or others. They may even tell you that this isn't what they are doing even when it is.

It is often difficult for a spouse to feel safe and vulnerable when there has been involvement with pornography or addiction because this is often seen as an attachment injury or rupture, which can be just as threatening as an actual physical threat to safety. Even when one is confident that one's spouse is sober and not using sex to act out, it may be difficult for the traumatized partner to feel safe and vulnerable. I recommend open and honest communication prior to intimacy, when the traumatized spouse is triggered during intimacy, and after a sexual encounter. Do not allow the addiction to continue to ruin your lives by being frustrated that sex needs to take a time out in order for you and your spouse to talk and ensure that your partner feels safe. You will find that with time, your relationship will be stronger than ever before by working as a team to eradicate the remnants of the addiction in your sexual relationship. Remember that the pornography is just the tip of the iceberg. The bases of the iceberg or root issue are things like holding back vulnerability, isolation, selfishness, and poor communication. These are character weaknesses that require change for a foundation of healthy sexuality. Additionally, such changes will produce healthy relational and sexual dynamics for the couple.

No matter what the progress in recovery, the addict needs to do a complete disclosure to his or her spouse to discontinue injury. Every time spouses find out a new piece or element of the addiction, they are reinjured. This reinjuring is disastrous, which makes it more and more difficult for the couple to have a fulfilling sex life. The spouse will find it increasingly difficult to want such vulnerability and interaction. Once this disclosure takes place, the couple can really begin healing and building a healthy sex life.

What all of this requires is a lot of communication before, during, and after sexual intimacy. Accessible, responsive, and engaged spouses (or "ARE") are what attachment expert Sue Johnson says rebuild security and vulnerability in a relationship.[3] Sex is easier to do than to talk about. When a sexual addiction has been involved, communication is even more important. Increased communication and adaptability are vital.

SEXUAL PERFORMANCE

With addiction or out of control sexual behavior the brain can change size and form. When the brain makes any kind of change in size or form its called neuroplasticity. With addiction or out of control sexual behavior neuroplasticity can cause the dopamine receptors to shrink. These receptors may not be back to normal, depending on the stage of recovery. Research has recently shown these changes in the brain to be associated with a correlation to erectile dysfunction or performance issues. The frontal lobe, or the brakes of the brain, also shrinks. Neuroplasticity has been shown to take place with those that have had addictions. With months of recovery, these damaged areas can regain their size, both in drug (methamphetamine)[4] and in natural (obesity)[5] addictions.[6] Additionally, sexual conditioning to certain stimuli, produces erectile dysfunction or anorgasmia when the stimulus changes. This means that the addict has conditioned himself or herself to sexually perform to pornography and masturbation, thus making it difficult to sexually perform with partner intimacy.

If erectile dysfunction is a result of sexual addiction, the couple will need to be adaptive. It may be that he can manually stimulate his spouse, that the couple can cuddle and bond emotionally, or that they can enjoy mutual sensual and sexual touch without intercourse. Essentially, they roll with the punches. They can also do the "start-stop method," which is described in detail in the chapter "Common Questions & Solutions" (Kaplan, pg 28).

The great thing about sexual conditioning is that it goes both ways. Yes, people can condition themselves to respond sexually to images on their phone and to self-touch. However, they can also condition themselves to respond sexually to vaginal intercourse, a partner being present, and bonding or connection. The couple can begin this by weaning the addicted spouse from his or her cues for sexual performance. Obviously, pornography or self-stimulation will not be used to do this.

Let's discuss a case where the husband has erectile dysfunction due to conditioning. Since he is used to manual stimulation for performance, the couple can begin there. Erection can be gained by the husband placing his hand on top of his spouse's hand and directing her touch. He should orgasm this way at the beginning of the reconditioning. As some time goes on, he should remove his hand from his spouse's hand and allow her to stimulate him to orgasm moments before he reaches climax. With time, he will remove his hand from hers farther and farther away from orgasm. They are to do this until she is the one stimulating him throughout the entire process. Next, the wife provides manual stimulation to the husband's penis near the point of orgasm, and then the couple switches to intercourse. Orgasm may or may not occur at this point for him. The couple then progressively switches to intercourse sooner and sooner, until minimal to no manual stimulation is needed to attain intercourse and vaginal orgasm. It is easiest for the husband to be lying on his back and the wife to be pre-lubricated when she stimulates him in this way. When they are ready to switch to intercourse, the wife gets on top of the husband and is in control of inserting his penis. In this way, the husband can relax and enjoy the pleasure, thus eliminating distractions that can lead to erectile dysfunction.

Many partners of addicts discuss the fear of being objectified or the fear that sex is just a way for the addict to act out. It is needless to say that any trace of this must be eradicated. Even if the addict isn't objectifying his or her spouse, the fears of the spouse need to be honored, heard, and put to rest in a respectful manner. Sometimes the addict may be unaware of the ways that he or she is objectifying the spouse. It is important for sex to be an option and not a need. If you are seeking out sex because you feel as though you need it and cannot imagine going through another day without it, you are probably using sex to act out. If you as a couple are not having sex or are having sex very infrequently, these feelings may have some validity.

Addicts should also evaluate their focus and mind-set while engaged in intercourse. If they are going through the motions with limited engagement and connection, there is a chance that they are using sex to act out. Additionally, a partner may feel that the addict is using sex to act out if the addict hasn't been putting into practice emotional foreplay as discussed earlier. Neglecting to do emotional foreplay doesn't mean that you are using sex to act out; however, your partner may feel that it does. Please be mindful of this.

If addiction hadn't been present in your life, you may have gotten away with not working on this. You wouldn't have been better for it, however. Now that the addiction has been present to some degree or another, you will need to change how sex is done in a very fundamental way. This will be individual to each of you as a couple. I will add a few areas that should be addressed concerning this in the activity section below.

Sex will need to change because the addict has brought into it some very unhealthy sexual practices and patterns, wittingly or not. A great example of this is a couple whom I used to meet with. Both partners had an addiction and had identified that they didn't have a clue about healthy sexuality. They didn't know what was normal to think or say. They didn't know what was appropriate for initiating sex or under what circumstances to initiate sex. It is needless to say that they struggled immensely with knowing how to engage in a bonding sexual experience. While you and your partner may not struggle to this degree, you can see that there are ways that media, pornography, and sexual scripts can creep into your sex life in various forms. One such minor degree would be expecting a woman or man to want a certain kind of sex just because of their biological sex. Media portrays women yearning for rough penetrative sex, when this is by no means a standard. Similarly, media portrays men as devaluing soft, connecting, and loving intercourse.

ACTIVITY

Your assignment for this section is to talk about the differing dimensions of healthy sex. Areas might include in what circumstances it is OK to seek sex out, what should be said or thought during sex, what makes sex a bonding and connecting experience, and what sexual practices should be included in healthy sex. Fortunately, you most likely have a spouse who knows what healthy sexuality should include. Work together on figuring this out for the two of you and begin implementing these changes.

NOT ALL UNWANTED SEXUAL ACTIVITY IS A SEXUAL ADDICTION

Many wonder if their sexual activity constitutes a sexual addiction. Mental health therapists use the Diagnostic and Statistical Manual of Mental Disorders (DSM), most recent version 5, to diagnose clients. The authors of the DSM have never included a diagnosis of sexual addiction in any of the editions of this very large text. Some therapists diagnose clients with other DSM diagnoses such as conduct, OCD, or compulsive and impulsive diagnosis, when the criterion fit and are ethical. Now this doesn't mean that a sexual addiction doesn't exist. However, it merely means that the authors and contributors to the DSM have found inconclusive evidence of such a diagnosis.

After gaining a taste for academia, I know that some researchers have an agenda. This may or may not be a contributing factor in leaving out the sexual addiction diagnosis. I'm unsure since I do not know the authors and contributors of the DSM personally. I also know that a sexual addiction diagnosis would pathologize many that find nothing wrong with pornography, masturbation, virtual sex, frequent and vast sexual encounters with no attachment, or extramarital relationships of all forms, for example. In fact, many individuals that otherwise feel they have a healthy and robust sex life might meet criterion for a sexual addiction diagnosis should one be included. Creating a sexual addiction diagnosis also would purport that there is "normal" sexual behavior that all humans should engage in, and then unnatural sexual behavior. This would marginalize and pathologize individuals that do not fit within this "norm" of sexual behavior. Additionally, those that engage in the before mentioned may not even be considered addicted since they might not meet the entire criterion for such a diagnosis such as the behavior causing distress in relationships.

I know that many in our culture pathologize their own sexual activity if it doesn't meet LDS sexual values such as viewing pornography and sexual activity outside of marriage. Instead of seeing those activities as counter values these are often seen as pathological. While I do not profess to state what is right or wrong here, I do know that many great members of our faith resign themselves to a self-diagnosis of sexual addiction when in fact they may not meet the more accepted sexual addiction criteria put forth by one of the prominent sexual addiction researchers in the field, Patrick Carnes. I have chosen to include Carnes's criteria here:[7]

- Recurrent failure to resist sexual impulses to engage in specific sexual behavior
- Frequent engaging in those behaviors to a greater extent or over a longer period of time than intended
- Persistent desire or unsuccessful efforts to stop, to reduce, or to control behaviors
- Inordinate amount of time spent in obtaining sex, being sexual, or recovering from sexual experiences
- Preoccupation with the behavior or preparatory activities
- Frequent engaging in the behavior when expected to fulfill occupational, academic, domestic, or social obligations

- Continuation of the behavior despite knowledge of having a persistent or recurrent social, financial, psychological, problem that is caused or exacerbated by the behavior
- Need to increase the intensity, frequency, number, or risk of behaviors to achieve the desired effect or diminished effect with continued behaviors at the same level of intensity, frequency, number, or risk
- Giving up or limiting social, occupational, or recreational activities because of the behavior
- Distress, anxiety, restlessness, or irritability if unable to engage in the behavior

Whether you meet these criteria or not, you might be experiencing distress from your sexual behavior. Just because your behavior doesn't meet these criteria doesn't mean that it isn't significant or that it doesn't need to be altered to fit your values or your relationship expectations. I urge you to take the space below and think about your unwanted sexual behavior. Does it fit the diagnostic criteria stated above? If not, does it cause distress to you or your partner? If so, what would a healthy version of your sexual behavior look like?

*What do you need to be **attentive** to from this chapter?*

*What do you need to be **accountable** for from this chapter?*

_____

_____

*What do you need to **accept** about this chapter?*

_____

_____

*What needs to be **re-storied** from this chapter?*

_____

_____

_____

⚜ Notes ⚜

1. Jeffrey R. Holland, "Of Souls, Symbols, and Sacraments" (Brigham Young University devotional, Provo, UT, 1988), http://emp.byui.edu/WARDD/honors221/articles/souls.htm.
2. William Simon and John H. Ganon, "Sexual Scripts: Permanence and Change," *Archives of Sexual Behavior* 15, no. 2 (April 1986): 97, http://doi.org/10.1007/BF01542219.
3. Sue Johnson, "Shaping Love: A Seminal Study," DrSueJohnson.com, accessed Oct. 24, 2017, http://drsuejohnson.com/science-2/shaping-love-a-seminal-study/.
4. Seog Ju Kim et al., "Prefrontal Grey-Matter Changes in Short-Term and Long-Term Abstinent Methamphetamine Abusers," *International Journal of Neuropsychopharmocology*, no. 9 (2006): 221–28, doi:10.1017/S1461145705005699.
5. Lauri T. Haltia et al., "Brain White Matter Expansion in Human Obesity and the Recovering Effect of Dieting," *Journal of Clinical Endocrinology & Metabolism* 92, no. 8 (2007), 3278–84, https://doi.org/10.1210/jc.2006-2495.
6. Donald L. Hilton Jr., *He Restoreth My Soul: Understanding and Breaking the Chemical and Spiritual Chains of Pornography Addiction through the Atonement of Jesus Christ* (San Antonio, Texas: Forward Press Publishing, 2009), 63.
7. Patrick Carnes, "Sexual Addiction and Compulsion: Recognition, Treatment, and Recovery," *CNS Spectrums* 5, no. 10 (2000): 66.

MYTHS about
SEXUAL INTIMACY

One of my favorite things that I get to do in therapy is to dispel myths. Myths are created and instilled in us from a very young age about all things—yes, even about sexual relationships. Despite myth-busting facts, statements, or anecdotal tales, these myths have a way of hanging on. It's not so different from the myth that there is one specific person for everyone. Contrary to counsel that this myth isn't true,[1] I still find men and women searching for this perfect person. So as you read about the sexual myths that our LDS cultural society—as well as the larger society—portrays, try to challenge your beliefs about these myths and work on dispelling them.

Myth #1: Men are always ready and capable of having sex at any time with anyone. Society would wrongly have women and men think that men are sexual machines. Men are not capable of having a firm enough erection for sex at the drop of a hat. They are not built this way, thankfully. It's true that in some circumstances, a full and firm erection can be had by your partner right when you say you are ready for intimacy. Most often this is because they feel close to you, because they desire to feel connected, or because they have been fueling sexual thoughts all day long. When this happens, great. Men do, on average, take less time than women to be sexually aroused. This has to do with their self-sexual programming, which was discussed in the previous section.

So men have the appearance of being sexual machines. This doesn't mean that there won't be times when the wife is more quickly aroused than her spouse. The danger with this myth is twofold. For men, they can take to heart an instance when they are not fully aroused, when they lose their erection, or when an erection takes longer than they want. This can then give rise to concern that the same will continue to occur, thus leading to what they fear the most. For women, they can see themselves as inferior sexually or as incapable of great sexuality just because they might take longer to get aroused. This negative schema can be detrimental and squash any arousal that they feel.

Myth #2: Whenever there is a sexual dysfunction, it's a red flag, and you should take it seriously. Research shows that within a healthy couple's sexual relationship there will be what can be defined as sexual dysfunction from time to time. Don't let this get to you or your partner. Allowing yourself to dwell on the times that you couldn't perform will be your downfall. No guy is going to talk to his buddies about his latest sexual encounter being a bust. Men typically don't want to let other men know about their vulnerabilities, especially if society has a perception of them that is radically different from what they are going to say. Can you imagine a man telling his friends during a game of golf that he wasn't able to get an erection the night before or that he couldn't have an orgasm?

When a sexual dysfunction occurs, don't let this get to you or your spouse. Simply roll with the punches and continue whatever makes you and your partner feel good sexually. By stopping the sexual encounter and getting frustrated and upset, you let the dysfunction become larger than it really is and become more prominent than it should be. By wrongly and disproportionately focusing on the dysfunction, you may engender a more pervasive issue. The anxiety that the dysfunction is going to happen again usually engenders just that. How could it not? When you are trying to have sex and your mind is focusing on keeping an erection, you have become a spectator to your erection, which is not arousing. If this issue happens more than every once in a while, or if rolling with the punches doesn't take care of the problem, contact someone who specializes in sex therapy or a medical doctor.

Myth #3: The best time to have sex is when you crave sexual touch. Society has also played a nasty trick on couples concerning sexual desire. Society has taught us that desire is all about wanting a physical encounter centered on physical pleasure. This is incorrect, especially for women. It is perfectly normal for both husband and wife to desire sex because they feel close or want to feel emotional connection and closeness in the absence of physical arousal. It could also include wanting to show devotion or love or wanting to partake in the sacrament of marriage (marital sexual intimacy). Desire for the physical reward of the sexual encounter or climax is also a very viable reason for women, just as it is for men, to seek out intercourse. From this time forward, own any sexual desire that you feel and do not rank it.

Myth #4: Sex is going to be painful. While some women experience some discomfort or even pain the first few times they have sex, sex should not be painful when performed correctly. If the hymen is still partially intact, there could be some pain at the onset of the sexual relationship. After having sex a few times, the thin membrane should be completely removed. There are a few reasons why a woman with no abnormal physical or pharmacological issues would have pain or discomfort. If there isn't enough arousal or lubrication, sex can be painful. The lack of arousal prevents the female body from doing what it needs to do in order to feel good during sex. When sufficient arousal takes place, the vagina lengthens and expands to accommodate the man's penis. If there is not enough arousal because sex was rushed and not enough time was spent in foreplay, then pain or discomfort may be present. Additionally, nervousness or anxiety can engender pain or discomfort because the muscles in the vaginal canal are tense and tight and the vagina hasn't lengthened and expanded properly. This anxiety can be brought on out of fear that sex is going to hurt or because there is a medical or pharmacological cause that has since been taken care of. Let me explain.

Let's say that a certain medication was causing vaginal dryness, and the couple found this out after they had been having sex for a few months. Sex to that point had been painful and wasn't enjoyable. However, after the medication was changed and there was no longer vaginal dryness, the woman still experienced pain during sex. This subsequent pain could be due to the fact that she was unable to relax the vaginal canal because she was still fearful that sex would be painful. This could all be a subconscious process that required her to increase awareness and utilize relaxation techniques.

More often than not, sex should not be painful or uncomfortable for the woman. I have seen the inverse message to be more of a self-fulfilling prophecy than anything. Pain or discomfort during sex is not usually an issue for men. I have found that where parents, friends, peers, and leaders have taught women that sex is enjoyable, pleasurable, fulfilling, and satisfying, women are less likely to develop any type of sexual pain disorder than women who have been taught that sex is painful.

Imagine that you were told by all those you trust and love that your marriage was going to cause you a great deal of pain and that sexual pleasure was only for your spouse. All of these loved ones had experienced a marriage and had felt this pain and seen their spouses find joy in the marriage where they hadn't. I imagine that there would be very little reason to disbelieve them, right? So the time comes that you get married. What might you be thinking and feeling? Would you be guarding your emotions and vulnerabilities? You hold back in the relationship and try to protect yourself but to the determent of a happy marriage.

To a degree, this is what women face when told inaccurate messages about sex being painful. Their bodies and minds are not in a place to enjoy the sexual encounter or to receive sexual pleasure. The vagina is tense and rigid. There hasn't been sufficient arousal, lubrication, or transformation of the vagina during the foreplay act for penetration to be pain- or discomfort-free or even pleasurable. The messages told to them by all of their trusted loved ones end up appearing true. Sex is not fun, and it's not for them, they think. We do a tremendous disservice to the ones we love by conveying these inaccurate messages.

Myth #5: A similarly false message that I have seen, not only from our smaller LDS society but also from society in general, is that sex is for the man. This statement is incredibly inaccurate. When the thought of this is given to men and women, sex does become about the man. Women who are taught that sex is as much for them as it is for their husbands find a great amount of pleasure in their sexual relationships. Both husband and wife need to advocate for the woman's sexual experience, although we as individuals need to be the biggest advocates for ourselves. Find what does create the most sexual fulfillment or arousal. Is it time, technique, closeness, taking charge? Each individual is different, and we need to take charge of exploring what it is that increases our sexual experience.

Myth #6: Something is wrong if you are a man who doesn't crave sex or if you are a woman who does crave sex. While I've alluded to this, I want to directly address women and their sex drives, or the libido. The longer I practice sex therapy, the more I meet with women who do not fall within the stereotypical norm. The stereotype for a long time was that women are less sexual than men. I have met with plenty of women who dispel this myth. I would still say that women generally have less of a sex drive than men. However, there are those women who are in therapy because they want to have sex way more than their husbands do. Similarly, there are plenty of men who aren't the stereotypical male (who only thinks about sex). The most important thing to take from this is that it's OK if you are one of those women or men who does not fit in your gender's stereotype; embrace who you are and that you are more or less sexual, and make it work for your relationship. By seeing yourself as abnormal or weird, you could hurt your sexual satisfaction and sexual self-perception.

Myth #7: Another myth that is fun for me to bust is that sex in life is like it is in the movies or romantic books or as it is portrayed in pornography. There are many different dimensions that make sex dissimilar to what the media would have us believe, but I will just touch on a few. First, the man or woman is not always going to be sexually aroused enough to have intercourse a few moments into the sexual encounter. It may take him a few minutes to gain a hard-enough erection for penetration. Similarly, it could and will most likely take her some time for arousal to be strong enough for enjoyable penetration. Second, the sexual encounter is not a disaster if it's less than earth-shattering. It takes time and work to be able to orgasm during sex. Third, sex does not need to end in intercourse and simultaneous orgasm. Enjoyable sex may or may not include intercourse. Sex is very broad.

Do not allow media portrayals to limit your perception of sex. Simultaneous orgasm is definitely possible and enjoyable when it happens, but do not be discouraged if you and your spouse do not orgasm at the same time or if your sexual encounter doesn't lead to intercourse. One spouse having an orgasm and the other not or having an orgasm at a different time is more typical than simultaneous orgasm. These myths in media about sex are really irrational thinking. For example, it's irrational to think that the man is going to have nothing on his mind but sex all of the time and that at any moment when sex is possible his erection is going to turn from soft to hard in the time it takes to take off both parties' clothes.

Myth #8: Another false statement about sex is that one needs to have an orgasm to have a satisfying sexual experience. This is absolutely false for both men and women. The world makes us feel as if this is the case, but it doesn't need to be. Many men and women describe very sexually satisfying experiences that are void of an orgasm. What makes a sexually satisfying experience is having a large amount of pleasure, not an orgasm. This pleasure could come in terms of sensual, sexual, or emotional pleasure. Much research and writing in the world of sexuality is focused on pleasure and not orgasm. It states that the goal of sex should never be intercourse and should absolutely never be orgasm. The goal of sex should be to do whatever increases the sensual, sexual, and emotional pleasure felt by and between partners. In general, men find more sexual satisfaction from having an orgasm, but this isn't a must or a rule.

Myth #9: Women love to have their breasts and nipples touched, sucked on, or played with. Not all women like breast and nipple stimulation. For the most part, women need to be in the right mood or mindset for either breast or nipple stimulation to be sexually pleasurable or even bearable. Nipples have many nerve endings on them that can make stimulation uncomfortable. Breast stimulation can feel good to women, but probably not as good as most men imagine. It will most likely do more for the man than for the woman. For some women, breast and nipple stimulation begins to feel sexually pleasing when they have progressed to a further stage such as the arousal and orgasm stage, or when the woman decides to be open to arousal depending on the sexual response cycle that best fits. While breast and nipple stimulation may not bring your spouse to orgasm alone, it can be very pleasurable or can augment the experience. Similarly, testicle stimulation can be very enjoyable for some men.

This can be a great opportunity for conversation and exploration with your spouse. Talk with your spouse and explore what feels good and where. You may find a newfound sexual button to increase sexual fulfillment. Remember, sex is about far more than just penile-vaginal penetration. When you engage all of your senses, such as stroking your partner's hair and feeling or noting their erotic breathing, you will begin to partake of the full sexual experience, not only what's happening below the belt.

Myth #10: Only attractive men and women can be sexual. The sexual scripts that we glean from media, pornography, peers, and family wire our sexuality with the scripts that are being portrayed through these and other sources. In a society that is heavily sexually scripted by media and pornography, we glean certain messages about who can and should be sexual and to what extent. One such script is that only hot or attractive people can be sexual. We have limited scripts that the shapely women, thin man, small breasted women, man with below average size penis, elderly, ill, mentally ill, over-weight, or unattractive can be sexual. This is just not true. It suppresses and marginalizes these and other groups. If you happen to fit in the definition of those that are attractive and young then it also impacts you as well. For many of us, staying within this category becomes ever so important as anything else takes away your sexuality. However, this end is impossible. I have seen truly beautiful people surrender their sexuality because they do not feel they any longer fit within society's script for what is hot and therefore feel gross wanting or enjoying sex. The focus needs to be more on how we feel rather than whether or not we fit into a certain category that deems us "sexy or not". We need to broaden the concept of sexy to include different body sizes, skin and hair color, age, financial status, education, hip-to waist ratio, erotic preferences, penis size, accents, and so on.

Myth #11: A sexual addiction will give rise to some type of sexual dysfunction or issue in the sexual relationship. Over the course of my career, I have had many men and women who come to therapy for a sexual dysfunction, convinced that their teens and twenties, consumed by a sexual addiction to pornography and masturbation, are the cause for their premature ejaculation, low sexual desire, pain, erectile dysfunction, anorgasmia, or lack of sexual satisfaction. While their fear is not unfounded, some of their extreme focus and fear actually gives rise to the dysfunction or low satisfaction that they experience.

There is recent research that correlates sexual addiction to erectile dysfunction, as the brain is altered with such addiction. Similarly, individuals who have programmed their bodies to sexually respond to a very specific ritualistic behavior, like masturbating to pornography, might possibly have issues performing with a partner or finding fulfillment. However, this may not always be the case. With recovery, the brain can change back to a healthier state.

Even in the case of sexual addiction, the addiction does not singularly meet the criteria for erectile dysfunction to begin. More often the anxiety about the sexual addiction causing some type of dysfunction is more damaging than the sexual programming or performance impact of the addiction. My encouragement would be to get into recovery, if you haven't already, and allow the body and mind to heal. Have a healthy sexual relationship with your spouse. Do not use your spouse to feed your addictive tendencies. There might be some adjustment needed to this new way of behaving sexually. These may not exist at all or may be minor if you are both able to be a team and adapt.

◈ ACTIVITY ◈

Your first activity for this chapter is to separately write down all of the sexual myths that you hold concerning sexual intimacy. Next, talk with your spouse about these myths. Which ones impair your sexual relationship? Which ones have caused a negative pattern in your sex life? How can you begin to work on these? What can you both do to create more truth about sexual intimacy for your children?

Your second activity is to discuss the following questions with one another:

- What brings me the most sexual pleasure?
- What *do I do* when there is a sexual issue or dysfunction for me or my spouse?
- What *should* I do when there is a sexual issue or dysfunction for me or my spouse?
- What brings me sexual desire? List multiple categories (touch, connection, fantasy, etc.).
- How can I embrace my own level of sexuality in marriage while promoting the relationship?
- How has media impacted my view of gender, sexuality, and sexual capability? How has it impacted my view of my spouse's gender, sexuality, and sexual capability?
- How do I feel when only one or neither of us has an orgasm during sex, or when sex doesn't include intercourse?
- How do I feel about breast and nipple stimulation?
- How often have I viewed pornography or masturbated in my life and in the last three months? If addicted, how is this impacting my sex life and sexual safety?
- Men: Why and how often do I rush to sex before my partner is appropriately aroused?
- Men: When have I not been appropriately aroused for sex, and what has been my comfort level in talking to my spouse or letting her know?

- Women: How sexually capable do I feel in relation to my spouse and in relation to other women?
- Women: Why and how often has sex been painful or uncomfortable?

*What do you need to be **attentive** to from this chapter?*

_____

_____

*What do you need to be **accountable** for from this chapter?*

_____

_____

*What do you need to **accept** about this chapter?*

_____

_____

*What needs to be **re-storied** from this chapter?*

_____

_____

❧ NOTE ☙

1. See "Is There Such a Thing as 'Soul Mates'?" *New Era*, Nov. 2013, 48.

FACTS *about*
SEXUAL INTIMACY

F acts about sexual relationships are just as exciting for me to disclose to my clients as is dispelling myths. It's like I'm giving them keys to locks they were never able to open before. Sadly, they should have been given these keys long before finding their way into my office. I've compiled what I consider to be the most important facts about sexual intimacy—what every couple should know about sex but probably wasn't told.

Fact #1: Most women need direct clitoral stimulation to reach an orgasm. Intercourse, without much practice and education, usually doesn't provide the clitoral stimulation that a woman needs to reach an orgasm. I can't tell you how many times I have met with a newlywed couple where the wife explains her disappointment with and lack of pleasure in her sexual relationship. These women had hopes that sex was going to be emotionally and sexually pleasing and satisfying, but these dreams came crashing down when intercourse didn't provide the pleasure they once thought it would. This, combined with the negative view they have been fed about intercourse for women, leads them to believe that intercourse really isn't for the women.

In the chapter on gender differences, I discussed the need for clitoral stimulation and provided you with a sexual position and associated movement (CAT) that is the most effective for women to reach orgasm during intercourse. However, I didn't go into much detail about manual clitoral stimulation during intercourse. Some women may need to progress to the CAT from manual clitoral stimulation. There is an array of sexual positions that you can try as a couple where either you or your spouse can provide clitoral stimulation with a hand. Vaginal intercourse approached where the man penetrates the woman from behind allows either partner the ability to stimulate the clitoris. The man lying on the bed and the woman sitting on top can also provide her the ability to stimulate her clitoris while intercourse is taking place. The woman lying on her side with her legs spread apart where the man enters from behind and somewhat on top of her allows either partner to stimulate the clitoris. There are several others described at the end of the chapter called "Gender Differences."

Fact #2: Adaptability is one of the most crucial components for couples within their sexual relationship. Those who are adaptable report higher levels of sexual satisfaction and experience less dysfunction than those who are not. Adaptability can have many shapes and forms. One example is a couple where the husband has lost his once-vibrant sexual drive. A way for them to adapt would be finding ways for him and his wife to get their sexual needs and their desire for sexual, emotional, and physical closeness met. Another example might include new parents being more purposeful about planning their sexual intimacy, as they find that without planning and prioritizing, intimacy doesn't happen for them. Yet another could be a newlywed couple—surprised to find that sex is not as easy as they thought—reading books on marital intimacy or experimenting with sexual stimulation and positions until they find ways of increasing their sexual satisfaction.

While in the process of writing this book, a former client called and asked me what to do about the sexual issues she and her partner were having. She explained that she doesn't enjoy the positions that he is capable of engaging in and is at a loss for direction. She explained that her partner has a smaller penis that doesn't provide her with the type of stimulation that she enjoys. She is fearful that her life will be lived with low sexual satisfaction. With a little psychological education about sexual positioning, she felt hopeful, as I was able to provide her new positions that will give both of them the ability to enjoy sex. You see, there are positions that are for deeper penetration, for shallower penetration, for manual clitoral stimulation during intercourse, for couples during pregnancy, and the list goes on. Should the couple follow through, their adaptability will prove to be invaluable. A position that allows for deeper penetration includes the woman face down on the bed kneeling with her lower back arched. You can modify this position by using pillows under the woman's waist. She can spread her legs wider in either position and bring her knees or legs further under her. These allow for the vulva to be more exposed. Another position that allows for deep penetration includes the woman lying on her back with her legs spread open in a butterfly form, optional pillow under the small of her back for further exposure, may lying on top. The legs can be moved to on top of the man's shoulders, one leg brought up next to her head, or knees bent and brought up closer to her waist. This also makes it easier for the clitoris to rub against the man's pelvis or the woman can user her hand. Positions for shallower penetration include the woman sitting on top of the man lying on his back. She can then decide how deep she wants his penis to penetrate. An additional position includes standing face-to-face with the woman wrapping one leg around the man's upper leg while the man holds her leg close to her knee. The chapter titled "Gender Differences" and fact #1 in this chapter provide several positions for clitoral stimulation during intercourse. A great pregnancy position that also allows for clitoral stimulation by either partner is rear entry while lying in the spooning position.

Fact #3: As all of us age, there are crucial internal physical systems that are partially responsible for our sexual functioning that become less effective. The neurological, endocrine, and vascular systems are the three main sexual systems that simply become less effective as we age. The neurological system is responsible for all of the nerves, nerve receptors, and nerve endings that exist all throughout our bodies. The head of the penis and the clitoris have the largest concentration of nerve endings for men and women, respectively. When this system becomes less effective, touch that was once very stimulating becomes less so. The endocrine system is what manages our hormones. Hormones such as testosterone and estrogen are managed and maintained less effectively as we get older, giving rise to possible erectile dysfunction, pain, lack of lubrication, and lower sexual drive. The vascular system that is responsible for moving blood throughout our bodies similarly does a poorer job when we're older than when we were younger. As you might remember from the "Sexual Education" chapter, during arousal stages vasocongestion takes place, which is the large rush of blood to the sexual organs of the male and female. With this system operating poorly, engorgement of the clitoris and penis become more challenging. Because of this, it is vital that we do as was described above and adapt as couples to sustain our sexual satisfaction and ultimately our relational satisfaction.

Fact #4: Aging often necessitates a shift in how arousal occurs and is maintained. When younger, we may have relied on physiological process, such as touch to the penis or clitoris. When older, that same touch doesn't facilitate the sought-after arousal. A shift in building arousal is often needed. I'm not saying that physical touch isn't effective, just less effective than it once was. This is still a vital part of what brings about arousal for the couple. Subsequently, it will be important to focus on partner-interaction, self-entrancement, and role-enactment.[1] Partner-interaction includes engaging together during sex instead of going into one's head. Women typically prefer this to the other styles of sexual arousal. Looking into each other's eyes, allowing your partner's flirty smile to arouse you, or being in sync with breathing are all ways to use this style of arousal. Self-entrancement is most likely the dimension of arousal that will fade for both men and women as they age. Men typically prefer this dimension and will subsequently struggle until they can replace the reliance on this arousal style with one of the other two or a combination. Self-entrancement is going inward and building arousal based on the physical sensations you feel. Role enactment encompasses role play, incorporating new things into the sexual encounter, or the use of a sexual novelty item. I encourage the use of all three arousal styles for lifelong sexual fulfillment.

From time to time I will ask my clients if they look at each other in the eyes during sex or if they are turned inward toward their physiological sensations. It seems that more often than not couples can't remember what they do, at least at first thought. They usually follow this by saying that only rarely will they look into each other's eyes during sex. David Schnarch has coined the concept of looking into a partner' eyes during sex and orgasm.[2] Eyes-open sex and having one's eyes open during orgasm are ways for couples to go from self-entrancement to partner engagement. This can be a very telling activity as well. The couples that struggle doing this exercise often have some conflict in their marriage or have conditioned themselves to self-entrancement in order to perform sexually or have an orgasm. I encourage you to try to maintain eye contact with your spouse the next time you have sex and, more specifically, when you and your spouse have an orgasm. This can be a very bonding and connecting experiment, as you are most vulnerable during orgasm and intercourse.

Fact #5: With or without vaginal lubrication, sexual intercourse can still be uncomfortable or painful. I heard from a wise man once the principle of Occam's razor. Its basic tenet is that the simplest explanation is usually the right one. I have found this to be true within a couple's sexual relationship as well. There are many causes of sexual discomfort and pain for women. However, I find it best to start out by addressing the simplest explanation. Vaginal lubrication, as discussed previously, can reduce discomfort and pain during intercourse. However, sometimes the ways in which the lubrication is applied and the way that penile-vaginal penetration occurs can still engender discomfort or pain.

When applying lubrication, make sure to put enough lubrication on any part of the vagina and vulva that will make contact with the penis. This includes the labia majora and labia minora. The lack of sufficient lubrication can cause a rubbing and chafing for the woman that is distracting, unpleasant, and often painful. When the penis and labia make contact without lubrication or without enough lubrication, it will cause undesired friction that will only escalate as the man tries to push harder to get the penis to enter the vaginal canal or maintains thrusting. Additionally, when penetration occurs, it would be wise for the husband or wife to pull open the labia majora, and sometimes the labia minora, so that penetration can be smoother and reduce rubbing and chafing on the labia at the onset of intercourse. It's important to note that not all women need store-bought lubrication. Women naturally lubricate with arousal. However, this doesn't always mean that there will be enough lubrication or that lubrication will be in all the right places for pleasurable intercourse. Either partner can insert one finger into the woman's vagina and apply lubricant to the vulva or the head and shaft of the penis for ease of intercourse.

A little while ago, Molly and Oliver presented in therapy with the issue of anorgasmia for both partners. They determined, through me providing various starting point options, that they wanted to begin therapy with partner manual stimulation as a way to become orgasmic. Halfway into discussing a between-session activity, Molly stopped me and asked what I meant by manual stimulation. I realized that they hadn't seen, participated in, or had explained to them what manual stimulation was. While there are many ways to manually, with one's hand, provide stimulation to one's partner, I will describe what is typically meant. I will also describe manual stimulation of the woman.

For the woman to manually stimulate the man, she first clasps her hand around the man's penis. The tightness is for the man to determine and communicate to his spouse. She then strokes upward to the head of the penis and back down to the base of the penis in a rhythmic fashion. Varying speeds are also determined by the man and communicated to the spouse. As arousal begins, builds, and comes to a climax, the man may desire variations in the tightness and speed of rhythmic stimulation. Typically, the man will want slow, loose, rhythmic stroking at the onset and greater tightness and faster stroking with increased arousal. This was explained to the couple.

As has been described, women typically need to feel loved, cared for, safe, and cherished by the man prior to a sexual encounter. Their sexuality is typically broader than male sexuality. Many women desire a full body sensual caress that incorporates and progresses to touch of the breasts, nipples, and various parts of the vulva and vagina. It is advisable that the husband treats all parts of her body as sexual organs that have the capacity to exude sexual pleasure. A sensual tracing of her body or head rub can bring about a great deal of arousal. Integrate the touch of her vulva, vagina, and breasts while not focusing entirely on these until her sexual energy has increased. Shift the focus to a broad rubbing of the vulva from the top to bottom and back up, accentuating touch to the clitoris and taking note of what type of touch and intensity brings her more arousal. Some women enjoy manual stimulation where the man inserts his pointer and middle finger into the vagina with a rhythmic in and out movement or caressing of the interior of the vaginal canal walls. Other women enjoy a variation the aforementioned. Women should be vocal in directing their spouse's touch, intensity, and rhythm.

Molly and Oliver came back two weeks later and reported how their activity was for them. Oliver stated that it was nice but only with a loose grip. In that moment, I had another realization. They hadn't used any type of lubricant. It was explained to them that a lubricant is most often a must with manual stimulation, especially at the onset of a marital sexual relationship, when learning and programming is occurring. Without a lubricant during manual stimulation, the husband can often have chafing or undesirable rubbing, which is anything but pleasurable and will make orgasm very difficult.

Fact #6: It is fundamental for both partners to understand what they need in all areas of intimacy. I would like to address what this looks like in sexual relationships. Some partners have had sexual experiences before marriage, whether alone or with another person. In these instances, they are more likely to know what type of sexual stimulation they need at various times within a sexual encounter. For those who have not had such experiences or who do not know what type of stimulation they need, it is imperative that they discover this so that they can teach this to their partner. The couple should talk about ways that this can be done and how they feel about each avenue. It is encouraged that, whatever their choice, they should feel that it strengthens them as a couple and is not a result of selfish drives.

Avenues for sexual self-understanding can be found during a couple's sexual encounters. The wife can touch or explore her sexual anatomy with the aim of understanding and finding bridges to pleasure, arousal, or desire. Another avenue could be the wife doing this exploration and understanding while alone, without the pressure of an observer. It is vital that the couple feel that this is morally OK before the wife is to engage in this exercise.

A comfortable position for self-exploration includes the woman lying on her back with her knees bent. The woman should touch her vulva, the outside of the vagina, with a light touch. She can pull back the lips of the vagina to touch other surfaces, including the opening of the vagina, the vaginal canal, and the clitoris. She may need to pull back the clitoral hood to see the clitoris and provide stimulation. It is important for her to note that the clitoris may need a light touch while sexual desire and arousal are minimal and that firm, direct, or more rigorous touch may need to increase as sexual desire and arousal grow. Some women find that rocking, arching their back, thrusting their pelvis, muscle contractions, erotic or sexual breathing, engaging the pelvic floor muscles, or tightening the vagina around their finger can increase pleasure.

Fact #7: Sexual communication needs to occur to form a healthy sexual culture in your marriage. Something that couples often discuss in therapy are sexual noises or talk during intercourse. This is an essential component for couples trying to create a healthy culture around sexuality. That doesn't mean that noises or talking are a must, but the discussion of whether or not to have verbal expression during sex is a must. To some couples or individuals, this can be very distracting, and it takes them out of the sexual encounter, thus preventing them from progressing through the sexual response cycle. Other couples or individuals need or build off of sexual verbalization or hearing their partner's expression. Without the discussion of this topic, you and your spouse may be really missing the mark.

Should you have this conversation, you may find that your partner really enjoys when you talk sexually, comment on pleasurable moments, or moan during intercourse. You may in fact enjoy expressing this verbalization, and as a couple, you might both decide to increase this in your intimate relationship. This could be a very fulfilling part of your sex life. Remember, sex is about creating the most robust sensual, sexual, and emotional encounter possible. When this is done, you heighten all aspects of pleasure.

Fact #8: Intercourse can sometimes produce infections. If you have gone to the doctor before getting married for a premarital exam, you may have had the doctor or nurse talk to you about urinary tract infections (UTIs). These are sometimes known as honeymoon cystitis. Sex can introduce bacteria into the urinary tract of a woman. The bacteria then enter through the urethra and into the bladder. If not caught, this bacterium can get into the kidneys, causing infection and severe pain. Essentially, having sex places both partners—but especially the women—at risk of contracting a UTI. Scenarios that increase the likelihood of UTIs related to sex are when a woman first starts having sex and when sex is frequent. Urination before and right after sex, cleaning your genital and anal area before and after sex, and drinking water limit the likelihood of developing a UTI.

Fact #9: Individuals that have a relationship with their sexual anatomy are more easily able to tap into their sexual potential. When you embrace your sexual anatomy, your sexual potential goes through the roof. However, what I'm talking about here is more than embracing that you are sexual. The ideal is that each of us will develop a relationship with our sexual anatomy, whether that be a relationship with your breasts, vulva, vagina, clitoris or developing a relationship with your penis and testicles. I know it sounds a little strange at first, but hear me out. Those individuals that have had the greatest sexual expression and fulfillment are those that have developed this kind of relationship.

Mandy originally came to therapy because she had no interest in sex and didn't know how to enjoy it when it did happen. She wanted to make a change, but she didn't know how. She longed for sexuality to be a strength instead of a deficit. Mandy was one such client that went from being absent minded about her sexual anatomy to forming a really close relationship with it. When she came into therapy she was ambivalent about her vulva, vagina, clitoris, and breasts. When we talked about her sexual accountability, Mandy had a real wake-up moment. Two things came up for her. First, she realized that she had left her sexual awareness in her early days of youth. She remembered feeling embarrassed about thinking of sex and wanting to explore her body. She took familial and cultural messages of chastity to mean that she should avoid her sexuality. In so doing she left her budding relationship with her sexual anatomy behind. Whether that was the right or wrong thing for Mandy to do is up to her to decide, but at this point in her life not having a relationship with her vulva, vagina, clitoris, and breasts was obviously causing some issues in her life and with her spouse.

Second, she and her spouse subconsciously colluded to enable her sexual repression. Trent, her husband, was the caretaker of Mandy's sexuality by way of always initiating, being responsible for her satisfaction during sex, and through perpetuating the lie that *he* needed to get her in the mood. Mandy allowed him to enable her sexual repression by ignoring her sexual self. She expected her body to respond to Trent's and not have a voice of its own among many other unhealthy patterns.

Mandy began forming her relationship by writing and drawing her feelings of her vulva, vagina, clitoris, and breasts. She started to check in with them throughout the day. Mandy identified moments when she ignored their presence in her life. An example includes her ignoring how her nipples got erect—physiological arousal—when she would brush against the glass in their shower. Soon Mandy was aware of how often her sexual anatomy spoke to her. She found their voice when she would stretch her body and her clitoris would rub against her legs. She started speaking back by thinking such things as "I'm amazed by you. I'm grateful that you are telling me to shift my focus to my vulva for a moment. You make me feel, and I'm so alive when I feel." This new relationship with her vulva, vagina, clitoris, and breasts were the foundation of her sexual desire and shifting her sex life from relational deficit to a strength and context for connection and spirituality.

Fact #10: More progressive sex therapists are identifying that there is no pre-set or hardwired sexual response cycle (SRC) for men or women. These theorists posit that there are other "norms" for which individuals and couples experience sexual expression. The SRC that was described previously was used to more easily discuss what often takes place for women and men during a typical sexual encounter in terms of their physiological process. However, many women and men express and experience sex in a way that might not be stereotypical. For example, some women really enjoy penetration of all forms purely for penetration sake. Another example is that orgasm and intercourse is just one form of expression. Many healthy men enjoy experiencing erection and arousal without orgasm, or they find the process of being the object of their wife's sexual interest as the pinnacle moment of sex, over intercourse or orgasm.

By having a clear SRC, it creates an intercourse-centered scenario that discounts other forms of sexual expression or places these other forms of sex lower on the totem pole. The older SRC puts the focus of sexuality in a genital-centered way and not meaning-centered, where many couples actually find more satisfaction. Additionally, the older view actually ignores life cycle or discounts the sexual expression that occurs at different places in the life cycle or where medical or pharmacological constraints exist.

Fact #11: The only people that should determine healthy sexuality are the wife, husband, and God. Oftentimes couples look to others to determine what is healthy or what their sex life should look like. But only these three should determine such things as frequency, what sexual acts are okay or permissible, or what is too erotic or not erotic enough.

Fact #12: When there is not enough or too much erotic focus, individuals and couples struggle. As we all go throughout life, we can shift from non-erotic to erotic. An example is the man that goes for a jog and feels his penis bounce and jostle. He is aware of the beautiful women on the trail and their sexual anatomy as they jog along. He unwaveringly focuses on these aspects of these sexual others. He creates sexual scenarios in his mind of what could happen as he embarks on this run. This individual has become overly aware of the erotic world around him in this scenario. He may struggle with controlling sexual impulses.

Take another individual that goes for a jog. This man ignores his penis as it bounces and jostles. He ignores as it slightly fills with blood by the physiological arousal that takes place as his penile nerve endings rub against his clothing. He doesn't see the beautiful people around him. He also neglects to feel physically alive as he care-takes his physical form and it thanks him for this physical engagement. This individual is so absent to the erotic world that he may struggle with sexual desire.

Fact #13: We are on this Earth to get a body and have experiences in our bodies. I find that people struggle sexually when they fight one of the basic principles of the gospel. That is that we are on the earth to have body experiences. I firmly believe that God wants us to have experiences within our earthly bodies. Some of those experiences are of a sexual nature. There are a finite number of things that we can do with our bodies. One of the main things we can do is experience sexual pleasure with our spouse. When we try to neglect these sexual body experiences, we are being incongruent with one of the reasons we are upon the earth.

❧ *Activity* ❧

Your activity for this section is to teach your spouse about the type of manual sexual touch you desire. Women may struggle more with this, which is all the more reason to complete this assignment. You can show your spouse how to build your sexual arousal with manual stimulation. Then guide and direct your spouse through the process. This isn't intended for the purposes of having an orgasm. The intention is to understand what you need in order to go through the arousal threshold and, if desired, the orgasmic threshold. The arousal threshold is the continuum of slight to maximum level of sexual pleasure or arousal. Orgasmic threshold is the point in which high levels of arousal turn to orgasm. We each need to know our arousal and orgasmic threshold well enough that we can communicate it to our partner. It may take two, three, or many more times of teaching your partner. If you are unaware of what you need and enjoy with manual touch, your assignment is to explore this in a way that you and your partner feel comfortable with. Remember that your intention is for this knowledge and understanding to strengthen your relationship.

*What do you need to be **attentive** to from this chapter?*

_____

_____

*What do you need to be **accountable** for from this chapter?*

_____

_____

*What do you need to **accept** about this chapter?*

_____

_____

*What needs to be **re-storied** from this chapter?*

_____

_____

❧ NOTES ❧

1. Barry W. McCarthy and Michael E. Metz, *Men's Sexual Health: Fitness for Satisfying Sex* (New York: Taylor & Francis, 2008), 113–114.
2. David Schnarch, *Passionate Marriage: Love, Sex, and Intimacy in Emotionally Committed Relationships* (New York: W. W. Norton, 1997), 207.

COMMON QUESTIONS
& SOLUTIONS

This chapter includes what I have seen to be prevalent in my therapy practice. These are common issues, questions, insights, or roadblocks in sexual relationships. I will also include a step-by-step guide for a highly used sex therapy intervention: sensate focus. This is a tool that couples can use when there is anxiety, poor communication, dysfunction, lack of appropriate focus, inability to be present during sex, or low levels of satisfaction.

FEMALE SEXUAL PAIN

Vaginismus, or dyspareunia, is now called genito-pelvic/penetrative pain disorder and is one of the common problems for women that I see in therapy. Many of these cases have medical or physical origins. Others have pharmacological origins. Still others have psychological origins. Most often, no matter what the origin, there remains a psychological component that the couple needs to resolve. The woman is left feeling anxious that sex is going to cause pain because of these prior negative sexual experiences and therefore can't surrender to or enjoy foreplay, and the vagina doesn't adapt to accommodate the penis nor lubricate properly. What results is that what the woman fears—pain—leaves her even more despondent and resolved that sex will always hurt and be unsatisfying. As discussed previously, calming oneself, focusing on pleasure, and relaxing the vagina will facilitate pleasurable intercourse. To relax the vagina, the woman may need to do some preparatory work. After the cause has been identified and resolved, the woman can work through the residual psychological roadblocks to sex with a few simple exercises. See below.

Because this appears to be common, I feel it is important to address some interventions that the individual and the couple can do to combat this sexual intimacy assault. It is vital that you rule out any medical cause for the pain. Remember that a medical cause, even after properly dealt with, can still lead to sexual pain, as the wife is waiting for sex to be painful, causing a tightening of the vaginal canal and limiting arousal. One painful sexual encounter can also lead to ongoing sexual pain. That is, if the woman is unable to relax because she is fearful that sex will be painful, pain will still ensue.

The next several paragraphs will include a series of progressive exercises for female sexual pain. What I want you to think about and feel for is your comfort with these exercises. I only want you and your partner to engage in these exercises if they fall within your value systems. Anything that falls outside of your individual value systems will probably produce negative or insignificant results anyway.

DILATION FOR SEXUAL PAIN

The progression of these exercises begins with what we in the sex therapy world term *digital dilation*. This just means that the woman will use her finger to dilate her vaginal canal. To do this exercise, the woman places herself in a serene setting in which she will not be disturbed and feels that she is best able to relax. This may be in bed or on the couch, for example. She may want the room to be quiet or to have music on. Similarly, she may want the lights on or off. The goal is to create the most relaxing and comforting environment possible.

When conditions are ideal, the woman will begin by putting some water-based lubricant on her finger. For the sake of explaining this exercise, let's say that the woman is going to do this exercise on her bed. She may want to prop herself up or lie with her back on the bed. She will then bend her knees and rest her feet on the bed. Her goal is to start pairing relaxation of her pelvic floor muscles with inserting her finger into her vagina. To identify the pelvic floor muscles, she can pretend that she is trying to stop herself from urinating. This type of muscle flexing is what her pelvic floor muscles feel like when they are tightened. As she inserts her finger into her vagina, she wants to identify when she begins to feel tightening around her finger or discomfort. When she experiences this resistance, she is to stop her finger right where it is. Next, with her finger still inserted, she should try to tighten and relax those pelvic muscles that caused resistance upon finger insertion. Breathing deeply and purposefully with her eyes closed may help. Once her vaginal canal has relaxed and there is less or no tension, she can continue to insert her finger, doing this exercise without any resistance. Once this finger is fully inserted, she can do the same process with two fingers. When she is comfortable with the use of two fingers, she can move her fingers around inside of her vagina. She should pay attention to any tightening, working through this the same as when she experienced tightening before.

The next progression of the previously described exercise is to incorporate the husband into the activity. Remember, the wife will continue to be in control, so it won't be painful. With this progression, she will be in control of her partner's finger. He will merely provide her with the finger for dilation. She will guide his finger with her hand and stop it when she feels muscle tightening. Once she is able to progress through the use of both of his fingers with her being in control, she has finished this step.

The next step of the progression is to verbally talk to her partner and for him to pay attention to tightening surrounding his finger as he inserts one and then two of his fingers into the vagina. This concludes the use of digital dilation activity. The next step is to use synthetic dilators and progress through the series of synthetic dilators as you did with digital dilation. Dilators can be obtained from some doctors or can be found at various shops online.

The principles of the use of progressive synthetic dilators are the exact same as the principles used with digital dilation. Most couples prefer digital dilation. However, the use of synthetic dilation decreases the presence of a spectator, which makes it easier for some women to progress to the dilator size of a male penis more easily. Remember to use lubrication throughout this exercise as well. When the woman has been successful in using synthetic dilators to the size of a penis, she is ready to transition to intercourse.

When transitioning to intercourse, use the same slow movement of insertion as was described above. Once the man's penis is fully inserted, refer to the "quiet vagina technique" covered below (Kaplan, pg. 203).

Note that this technique can be used for multiple sexual problems. Slow and gentle movement is then next. The man is to lie on his back without moving. The woman, who is on top, is to engage in slow and gentle movement where she is entirely in control, stopping and relaxing her pelvic floor muscles when needed.

An aid to couples where there is premature ejaculation, or even pain upon intercourse, is a technique in sex therapy literature called the "quiet vagina technique." There are preliminary steps that the individual and couple can progress through with each problem, but I thought that it would be important to add this technique to this book. The woman pre-lubricates with a copious amount of water-based lubricant or almond oil (which will significantly reduce friction because it is extremely slippery). The woman mounts the man from on top, and neither partner moves. In the case of premature ejaculation, this helps the man become comfortable and desensitized to some degree with penetration without ejaculating. The man being on the bottom helps him to gain control and not have an orgasm. There are physiological reasons for this. In the case of pain during penetration, this technique will help the woman relax and get used to intravaginal penetration.

ADDITIONAL THOUGHTS ON DILATORS

Some exercises for women with female sexual pain would incorporate the use of a dilator. Medical doctors regularly prescribe a series of dilators to women who have such pain. The idea is that the woman can learn to have penetration with a device that simulates the size and girth of a penis while having all of the control and reducing spectatorship. What I have found is that most medical doctors prescribe this with a lack of follow-up and while neglecting some critical factors. If you are uncomfortable or feel that it conflicts with your value system, then you will not get the desired effects, and it won't be worth your time. If you can see this as a way to get to know your body and what your body needs in order to respond properly without having pain, as well as being an avenue for you and your spouse to connect and build your relationship, then a dilator is useful.

When using a dilator, it is important to be intertwined body and mind, to pair relaxation and penetration, to reduce performance demands, to use lubrication, and to learn control of the pelvic floor muscles. Many women will use a dilator because it was prescribed by a doctor all the while resenting the fact that they are using such a device. They will go through the physical motions and maybe even some of the other important features, like using lubrication and pairing relaxation, but they generally notice that it is still painful or impossible to have penetration. Here are a few reasons why that might occur.

Using a dilator properly starts long before the dilator is inserted vaginally, and it happens in the mind. A woman should be positively anticipating and looking forward to learning about this part of her body. If excitement about being alone in a relaxed setting where one can hone important skills for the relationship is present, then you are off to the right start. Keep in mind that, done correctly, this will *never* be painful. It should not be forced and should be done at the pace of the woman and her body. A relaxing environment, without kids banging on the door or your spouse as a spectator, is the ideal condition you will need. You need to allow for whatever time this takes you. You may need to dim the lights or put on relaxing music, but most important, take deep breaths and pair this with penetration. Reduce performance demands such as "I need to reach a certain point tonight" or "If only I could insert it more than halfway." You have most likely had few if any sexual experiences prior to sex with your spouse, so you haven't had the opportunity to learn throughout your life the ways of sexual performance.

Once more, there have been dominating messages that sex is going to be painful or uncomfortable. Allow your mind and body to embrace you as a sexual being at the rate that they need. More than likely, you will need lubrication on the dilator, on the vulva, and in the vagina. Use a water-based lubricant. Finally, your pelvic floor muscles are most likely tight. You need to learn how to tighten and loosen these. Remember, these are the same muscles used to stop the flow of urine. Practice tightening for three seconds and then loosening while the dilator is inserted. As you insert the dilator, go until you notice a tightening or until it becomes uncomfortable. You should practice tightening then loosening your pelvic floor muscles, and see if this allows for more movement of the dilator. Repeat until you are able to insert the entire dilator. Move up through the series of dilator sizes in this fashion.

ERECTILE DYSFUNCTION

Let's talk for a moment about erectile dysfunction. This can be a very embarrassing issue for men to have. In our society, men are made-up to be sex experts, which is unrealistic. I have met with many men, old and young, who struggle with this sexual dysfunction. Because of this commonality with many of my clients, I want to provide interventions that you and your spouse can begin using. A progressive set of exercises that have shown to be helpful for men struggling with erectile dysfunction will follow.

✎ ACTIVITY ✎

Before I begin describing it, I want to preface this exercise. This is the progressive set of sex therapy exercises that a sex therapist would use. You and your spouse need to assess what your level of comfort is with these assignments and determine where you might like to begin—your comfort level might begin at, say, step three and not the initial step. The first stage of this exercise begins with self-exploration and understanding. The man begins by stimulating his penis and testicles to find what is pleasurable and to increase that pleasure. Gaining an erection or having an orgasm is not the goal of this exercise.

The next step incorporates a technique called the "start-stop method," which is a mainstay of erectile dysfunction treatment. The exercise is meant to begin with the man alone stimulating his penis. The woman is not supposed to be present, since this causes external anxiety if there is a spectator. The man will stimulate his penis and do simply what is pleasurable. If an erection happens, continue for a minute, and then allow the erection to abate. When the erection is lost, go back through this step two other times.

The next step of this exercise incorporates the spouse. The wife is to stimulate her husband in the same manner. She is to start by touching the husband in a way that increases pleasure without the focus of him achieving an erection. If an erection appears, allow the erection to be present for a moment, and then she is to stop stimulating him until his erection abates. This is to be done three times. The man is able to orgasm if he and the wife agree at the end of the exercise.

SENSATE FOCUS

Sensate focus is a vital tool for all couples coming to sex therapy (Masters & Johnson, 1970). I would say that all couples should engage in sensate focus to continue to have a pleasurable and fulfilling sex life. This can be used throughout your lifetime to tune up your sexual relationship due to the comprehensive nature of its usefulness. I would like to cover some significant points of sensate focus. There are essentially nine reasons for sensate focus: increasing awareness of one's sensations, being attentive to one's needs, communicating sensual and sexual needs, awareness of partner's sensual and sexual needs, expanding sensual and sexual behaviors, appreciating foreplay, forming positive relational experiences, building sexual desire, and enhancing emotional intimacy.[1] Sensate focus has two phases: sensual and sexual. The couple should engage in these activities three times per week for twenty minutes each. During the weeks that you are progressing through sensate focus, intercourse is proscribed typically, but this is not a must. It all really depends on the reason for participation in sensate focus.

Stage one of sensate focus is sensual pleasure. It includes touching hands, feet, scalp, and face. This aids the couple in increasing verbal communication, creativity, and experimentation. The couple should make positive comments and have positive thoughts throughout the day leading to the encounter. The couple will progress from touch and massage of the aforementioned areas to touch and massage of all areas of the spouse's body, excluding genitalia, breasts, and buttocks. The assignment might only take one week but may take several weeks if the key principles are missed. The couple progresses when the level of comfort in giving nongenital, full-body massage is reached. Keep in mind that you need to be completely engaged and attentive to what the massage feels like. It isn't for you to relax and fall asleep to as you might with a typical massage.

Stage two of sensate focus is sensual pleasure with erotic stimulation of the breasts and genitalia. The couple is to start with nonsexual touch and move to prearranged sexual touch. They are to be aware of and interrupt negative cognitions. Orgasm is permitted but should not be the focus of this exercise. Graduated steps should be built into this phase, leading to any type of sensual and sexual touch outside of intercourse.

Stage three of sensate focus is transitioning to intercourse. The couple is to begin with nonsexual touch and lead into sexual touch. Intercourse is permitted, with prearranged penetrative intercourse as a possibility. If the spouse is not feeling like penetrative intercourse is going to increase pleasure, then he or she is not to follow through with the prearranged plan. The couple should use progressive steps with intercourse, for instance degrees of penetration—penetration without thrusting, or penetration without orgasm. The couple is to feel no pressure to or have a goal to orgasm or have intercourse. The main focus is to focus on sensations, positive thoughts, bonding, and fantasies.

COUPLE COMMUNICATION

There are books upon books concerning couple communication. Even books that are not fully about couple communication will go on for entire-chapter discussions about this component of the marital relationship. You can find links to these books at covenantsextherapy.com/book. I'm going to be brief in discussing this feature here. Couple communication is one of the most essential components in a relationship, and it significantly impacts relational satisfaction. It is a highly common element impacting the sexual relationship. I find that there is usually a breakdown in communication with most of the couples that come to therapy. Within their sexual relationship, there is even more of a plague related to couple communication.

Sometimes the culture that surrounds our faith explicitly, or more often implicitly, teaches that it isn't OK for partners to talk about sex, their sexual experiences, or issues in their sexual relationship. This is incorrect and will lead to significant sexual issues or lessened sexual—and undoubtedly relational—satisfaction. An article on the LDS *Church News* website addresses the impact of correct vs. incorrect sexual intimacy teaching: "'Misunderstanding healthy sexuality can have negative impacts on every other aspect of our lives, including our relationship with God,' said Howard Bangerter, product manager with Welfare Services who works on the Church's Overcoming Pornography website. Opposite of that, proper understanding can lead to joy and happiness in marriage and creating eternal families."[2] You as a couple need to be talking regularly about sex. You need to discuss things that you enjoy or dislike; your fantasies, concerns, hopes, and letdowns; any clarifying questions you might have; and so on. It is just as important to have the doors of communication open in this domain of your relationship as it is to have the doors of communication open in any other domain.

Most people have some form of anxiety to one extent or another. This could just be surrounding public speaking, new environments, or going to the airport. It is very clear that anxiety can play a significantly disastrous role in our lives. Most people do not experience anxiety to the extent that their lives are dramatically influenced, however. We typically see anxiety merely lessening our life satisfaction rather than destroying our lives. Anxiety can have a more impactful role in the realm of sexual intimacy than most would imagine.

Anxiety is, however, one of the largest contributors to sexual dysfunction. Anxiety in the sexual relationship looks much different than in other areas of life. This anxiety appears as negative anticipation (anticipatory anxiety), preoccupation, spectatorship, or monitoring—for example. The reason is that the anxiety takes us out of the experience, the pleasure, or the moment. In so doing, we are spectators. Being spectators to our anxiety and the sexual encounter is not arousing—thus decreasing our physiological responses as we take a departure from the sexual response cycle—and our bodies go back to the pre–sexual response cycle state, which in turn causes dysfunction. You as a couple need to become more comfortable with the fact that, until you work through your anxiety, you may have moments where the husband loses his erection—for example.

The loss of an erection is not an issue. An erection can return. The issue is the negative, defeating thoughts that will prevent you and your spouse from continuing or from feeling enough arousal to start again. If you as a couple are unable to communicate about your sexual encounters or experiences, then you will have more difficulty than need be. With the loss of an erection, the couple needs to adapt. Go from intercourse to foreplay. The husband can stimulate the wife, for example. You can make the appearance of a misfortune result in a more satisfying experience. When the erection returns, then intercourse can be engaged in again. It is all about what you do once you lose the erection, both personally and interpersonally. On the other hand, if you think negative, defeating thoughts about losing your erection, you are removed from the encounter. You then become a spectator as you wait and monitor your erection in the hope that it returns. It will most likely not return because you are too preoccupied with monitoring instead of enjoying sexual intimacy.

In my practice, I have worked with many newlywed couples struggling in their sexual relationships. One of the common issues that I encounter in therapy is erectile dysfunction in newlywed men. Upon working with these couples, I typically find that a few negative sexual encounters during the honeymoon or the first year of marriage have led to the more serious problem of erectile dysfunction. The men have on one or a few occasions lost or been unable to achieve an erection during foreplay or intercourse. This has engendered a great deal of anxiety in these men. They now enter into most of their sexual encounters with the fear or anxiety that they may not be able to gain or maintain an erection. In having this focus, they distract themselves from being in the sexual encounter. They are spectators to their erections. This is not arousing and actually prevents the important body messages being sent from the brain to the penis and associated internal structures that allow for the penis to fill with blood, expand, and retain this vasocongestion.

Some of the possible causes for them not being able to achieve erections initially could be that stress from work and school made it difficult for them to transition from their daytime responsibilities to the sexual encounters, or it prevented them from staying in their sexual encounters. Other times the loss of an erection has too much emphasis. Erections can come and go during a sexual encounter. Just as disproportionate focus on the need for erection can lead to erectile dysfunction, this same focus and anxiety from an encounter or two can lead to sexual pain, anorgasmia, or other sexual problems.

TRANSITIONING TO A SEXUAL STATE OF MIND

A common issue that couples face in their sexual lives is trying to move from a day where they have been immersed in work, parenting, or other activities into a sexual encounter. Unfortunately, it is not easy for most women to go from being a mother, who takes care of every need of two children all day, to seeing herself as a sexual being. Furthermore, it is difficult for that mother to want or desire sexual intimacy when she has not taken a second to take care for herself in even simple ways. The same can be true for men. A man who is up to his elbows in work and is bombarded by work calls, texts, and e-mails can find it difficult to engage in sex when his mind is on matters of work.

What I encourage both partners to do is to have a space for transition from the former role to a sexual role and encounter. Transitioning from the day can be difficult; most of the time it requires both mind and body to transition. Some individuals transition in a way that differs tremendously from others. Reading a book in the bath while knowing that a sexual encounter may transpire following it has helped many couples I have worked with. On the other hand, watching TV or getting something to eat while relaxing for a few minutes may be what others require to successfully transition from one role to another. Taking a few moments to decompress to a loved one, to close your eyes, and to lie down for a few minutes while you let go of the day and take in hopes for the night with your spouse may help others. The important thing to note here is that we often need a space or format in which we transition. Sex requires a tremendous amount of letting go and surrendering to pleasure and connection. If you are consciously or subconsciously stuck in your role as a parent, boss, employee, or friend, you will be hindered sexually.

SEXUAL FANTASY

For most LDS members, sexual fantasies are something that they tried hard to eliminate throughout their single lives. I'm by no means encouraging otherwise. However, I want to speak to the possible repercussions. When we cut this part out of our human experience, along with squelching sexual desire and arousal, our sexual identity and ability can decrease. We have in a way cut out sexuality from our human experience. When one gets married and is ready to have a sexual relationship, it can be difficult to regain this identity. Practice and deliberate attempts at fantasy must be made to reintegrate this aspect of sexuality into our everyday lives.

Some clients say that they don't want to have to try to desire their spouse or to fantasize. They don't want it if it's not naturally there. My reply is twofold. First, that it would be there if they would have nurtured it. Though I completely understand and honor why they didn't nurture it while they were not married. Second, this part of our existence is for growing and learning. We do not grow when we merely exist and only partake of those things that are easy. The good things in life never are easy.

Each spouse needs to fantasize about his or her partner. I encourage men and women to fantasize only about those things that they feel comfortable with. These fantasies should be deliberate throughout the day and should build desire, arousal, and connection. That leaves the door open for a vast array of fantasies. Highlight moments where you desire intimacy, sexual pleasure, or your partner. Take particular note of times when you are aroused and what brought that on. Learn to maintain and build this from the experiences you are now noting and embracing. This will take focus and effort at times. However, go into it with excitement and enthusiasm.

This is a note to pass on to single friends or for parents concerning personal connection to sexuality. To those unmarried individuals who don't want to lose their connections to their sexuality while still holding to their value systems, I would say accept, honor, and be grateful for sexual desire, arousal, and fantasy, but do not foster it. For example, for men, when a thought pops into your head about wanting to see an attractive woman naked, do not provoke and augment this, but acknowledge that it is normal, natural, and beautiful that you were given these divine drives to yearn for a sexual relationship with a woman. These same principles can be applied when you have an erection, for instance. Instead of trying to get the erection to go away and ignoring what it feels like, take a second to honor and accept this part of yourself, just as you did with the unprovoked sexual fantasy. When marriage comes along, you will have accepted this sexual part of yourself while staying true to your value system.

SEXUAL TONE

The sexual tone of a couple's relationship is more important than most realize. What I mean here is the vibe or feeling created by the couple during sexual expression. Many couples take on the sexual tone that is most familiar to them. This familiar tone could be from media, parents, past relationships, or solo experiences. Often times they are not aware that there are other options or that they have any control over the sexual vibe or tone.

The media and world portrays a view of sexual expression that is largely singular, meaning it illustrates that most people are having intercourse in certain positions, most people are focusing on the physical, or the man is most often the aggressor, for example. Essentially, it feels as though there is a right way and a wrong way to have sex or the typical or atypical way to express sexuality. Al Vernacchio in his TED Talk on sex provides a new helpful metaphor for sex. He discusses how the old metaphor of sex being like baseball is failing us. In the new metaphor, he describes there are no clear winners and losers. There is not a right or wrong way to experience sexuality. In the new metaphor, there is liberation from an old metaphor that was limiting and driven by pressure to perform and fit inside a "norm."[3]

Sometimes a couple will unwittingly take notes from their upbringing. They will translate the sexual expression (kissing, hugging, touching) they see their mom and dad engage in while in public into the couple's sexual relationship. What they don't realize is that mom and dad may have been very different while alone than in public.

The past sexual relationships that we have engaged in might set the tone for our future sexual relationship. If these were unhealthy or engaged in outside of marriage, these prior sexual tones may be fraught with shame, embarrassment, or non-connecting and spiritual aspects of sex that the couple may not want in their relationship.

Solo sexual experiences through masturbation, pornography, or otherwise may have more of an impact on the couple's sexual tone than many realize. In these solo experiences, one is not taking into account the other person and is experiencing sexuality in isolation. It is far more difficult for them to be vulnerable during sex, and it is different to have another person witness your sexual expression than when alone.

Two years ago, I was working with a man that was very loving and soft during sex with his wife. His wife was the same. They had assumed this sexual tone from their assumption about "What other LDS couples were doing during sex." The couple didn't really enjoy their sex life and at times avoided sex without really knowing the reason why sex felt so awkward. The couple soon began to realize that they were being sexual in all the ways that they felt were "right" and not what was right for them. The husband wanted to be more expressive and strong. The wife wanted to act sexier and be dominant at times. Once they were able to see this incongruence, the couple was able to intervene by being more authentic during sexual fantasy and couple sexual encounters. A few months later they had the sexual tone that was congruent for both of them. They found themselves looking forward to sex and making time for it because it was enjoyable and bonding.

ONE ISSUE CAUSES ANOTHER

A quick note about sexual dysfunction that I want to share is that one dysfunction usually engenders another dysfunction, either in one spouse or the other. So if the initial dysfunction or issue isn't enough to get you to work on your relationship, the potential of subsequent issues should be. To illustrate this, imagine a husband who has premature ejaculation. This sexual issue may cause such great anxiety and shame for the man that he now neglects sexual urges and fantasies of his spouse. Through time, this engenders low sexual desire.

To illustrate how this issue can engender a dysfunction in his partner, think of the same couple. The wife, being concerned about her husband and knowing that he feels emasculated by this, pays little attention to herself during sex. She is more concerned about her husband's experience. Through time she finds that she develops anorgasmia. Her anorgasmia is due to the fact that she cannot relax and enjoy sex. She is unable to focus on her own pleasure so much so that orgasm isn't possible without significant work.

While anxiety might plague some, I see simple cognitive processes plaguing others. Often the issue with performance or sexual satisfaction can be traced back to distracting thoughts during sexual intimacy. The husband may be too preoccupied with the long list of repairs he has to do or the dog clawing at the door, while the wife could be thinking of the newborn who will probably be waking up in the next couple of hours and the dinner she has in the oven. Thoughts like these are not arousing and will most often lead to sexual dysfunction and low levels of sexual satisfaction because the body and mind are intertwined. If the mind is not present during sex, the body will struggle as well. Eliminating these distracting thoughts and using thought replacement (described below) is key in overcoming these cognitive issues.

Thought replacement is the following: Couples I meet with are encouraged to journal distracting thoughts they have during sex, whether small or large. Sexually arousing and engaging thoughts are then written about. When the couple is being intimate and the husband is aware that he is thinking of something that has distracted him from enjoying sex before, he can quickly make this identification and kick the thought out of his mind. Following this, he is encouraged to replace the thought quickly with a sexually arousing or engaging one. Over and over again, the individual is encouraged to do these simple tasks until it is second nature and he can more readily stay in the act of sexual intimacy.

TYPICAL CONCERNS

I'm asked more than I can tell you what a "normal" couple's sexual relationship looks like. I describe two essential components here. The first I will term the level of sexual satisfaction. The second component is the frequency of intercourse. I usually begin by telling the couple that, within a normal, healthy sexual relationship—and I stress the term *healthy*—there will be amazing, earth-shattering sex, mediocre or OK sex, and some dysfunctional sex. One of the components of the "Good-Enough" sex model is the "85 percent" component. Where roughly 85 percent of the time couples will rate sex as very good, good, or fair 85 percent of the time and either dissatisfying or dysfunctional up to 15 percent of the time.[4] I repeat that they should expect some sexual dysfunction. This is what a healthy sex life looks like. So when you aren't able to have an orgasm, feel desire, or get an erection, don't overreact. It's probably just that part of your sexual relationship where there is a little dysfunction. If your dysfunction is persistent and causing real relational issues, then it's not part of a "normal, healthy sexual relationship." Seek assistance from a qualified therapist and bibliotherapy.

The second essential component is frequency. I don't like giving couples numbers, but I know that's what everyone is seeking. I want to first say that the couple should determine what is healthy and appropriate for them and not try to adhere to the sexual frequency that a national survey describes as "normal" or "typical." In national surveys looking at frequency of sex, there are different frequencies depending on age. If you are having sex one to three times a week, you are the large majority of couples.

A common question that I get in therapy is geared toward women having an orgasm during intercourse. Couples are curious if it is normal or typical for the woman to have an orgasm during intercourse. Typically, this has been a point of confusion for the couple, as they have heard varying things from friends, family, books, and elsewhere. They are also curious about the way that orgasm is achieved, from penetration or clitoral stimulation. The verdict on this is that, generally, women who have orgasms during intercourse are having an orgasm because they are receiving some type of clitoral stimulation. Those who do not have orgasms during intercourse are most likely struggling because the clitoral stimulation that they are receiving is either nonexistent, minimal, or not the right type. What causes a woman to orgasm during intercourse without clitoral stimulation is usually that the internal structure of the clitoris is being stimulated within the vaginal canal. With that being said, about 50 percent of women have orgasms during intercourse.

A common exercise for men and women struggling with sexual issues like anorgasmia, premature ejaculation, or even a low level of satisfaction is the Kegel exercise. Women have found it improves sexual pleasure as well as their ability to achieve orgasm. During intercourse, the woman should relax the pelvic floor muscles, which will allow for more comfortable intercourse. To do these exercises, relax the pelvic floor muscles, or the muscles you use to stop the flow of urine, and then slowly tighten and hold for three seconds. You can do a set of fifteen multiple times a day for several weeks. Strengthening these muscles may improve your sexual functioning and enjoyment.

All spouses will need to figure out how to orchestrate their arousal during a sexual response cycle. Orchestrating your sexual arousal during a sexual encounter means that you integrate those things that are highly, moderately, and minimally arousing in order to sexually perform as expected by yourself and your partner. Individuals who aren't able to appropriately orchestrate their sexual arousal might have an orgasm too early, might not build enough arousal to sustain an enjoyable sexual encounter, or might not even get themselves to a place with enough sexual arousal to engage in intercourse.

ACTIVITY

This will be your activity for this section as a couple. Both you and your spouse should write down those thoughts and behaviors that are sexually arousing. Next, rank them in order of arousal. Ideally, you would have things that fit into each level of arousal (high, moderate, and minimal). Finally, spend some time experimenting with your arousal continuum during sexual intimacy. Then discuss how the experimentation went. This list is the list that you can now draw from during a sexual encounter to meet the sexual arousal needed for penetrative intercourse, to stave off an orgasm so that your partner can enjoy sexual intimacy longer, or to bring yourself to orgasm. Remember that many things outside of simple sexual touch can be arousing and enhance the sexual experience. Use the space below for your thoughts:

What do you need to be **attentive** to from this chapter?

What do you need to be **accountable** for from this chapter?

What do you need to **accept** about this chapter?

What needs to be **re-storied** from this chapter?

❧ NOTES ❧

1. Gerald R. Weeks, Nancy Gambescia, and Katherine M. Hertlein, *A Clinician's Guide to Systemic Sex Therapy*, 2nd ed. (New York: Taylor & Francis, 2016), 158–162.
2. Marianne Holman Prescott, "How to Teach Children about Sexual Intimacy," *Church News*, March 16, 2015, https://www.lds.org/church/news/how-to-teach -children-about-sexual-intimacy/.
3. Al Vernacchio, "Sex Needs a New Metaphor. Here's one . . ." Filmed March 2012 in New York, NY. TED video, 8:18, https://www.ted.com/talks/al_vernacchio _sex_needs_a_new_metaphor_here_s_one/.
4. Michael E. Metz and Barry W. McCarthy, "The 'Good-Enough Sex' Model for Couple Sexual Satisfaction," *Sexual and Relationship Therapy* 22, no. 3 (2007): 357, http://dx.doi.org/10.1080/14681990601013492/.

PREMARITAL

M any people asked if I'd write a section in this book specifically to premarital couples and individuals preparing for marriage. Everything in this book can be applied to couples and individuals preparing for a fulfilling sex life. However, there are some unique aspects of an LDS person's sexuality that I thought would be helpful to include in this chapter. They are: shake off shame, foster a single person's sexual sense of self, learn self-care, develop sexual excitatory and inhibitory understanding and capability, and don't compare.

There is confusion about the differences of shame and guilt. Guilt says something about the behavior and shame says something about the person. Guilt is "I did something bad" and shame is "I am bad." In order to develop a healthy sexual self, a person needs to differentiate themselves from sexual shame. Shame can come from past sexual experiences, abuse, confusion or lack of information about sexuality, or misunderstanding about one's body. Where sexual shame exists, there is no place for sexual fulfillment. I have worked with many couples that try to make these two co-exist, and it just doesn't work. In order to find true sexual enjoyment, the shame has to be extracted.

EMMIE: A CASE STUDY ABOUT SHAME

Emmie had been dating a guy named Luke for the past three months. They were exclusive but she wasn't sure if she would marry him or not when I first started meeting with her. She was concerned that their sex life would be horrible if she did marry Luke. In fact, she was a little put off by the whole idea of marriage just because of her strange feelings about sex. This was difficult for her since she really did want to get married and have kids. Emmie had felt weird about her body since she became aware of her sexuality. To make matters worse, she was "flashed" by a boyfriend at age sixteen and had since been disgusted by the male body. Her boyfriend had exposed himself to her in hopes that she would want to have sex. She got freaked out by the whole ordeal and had really tried to avoid sexuality ever since. This was becoming increasingly difficult for her as she was getting older and hoped to get married some day. Not to mention that she really liked Luke and hadn't liked a guy this much before.

To help Emmie, we first had to eliminate the shame that she had over sexual anatomy. She had very little education or talks about her body and the male body. Emmie did some reading outside of therapy and looked at a few medical drawings and sketch art of the female and male form. We worked on processing through her emotions and where these thoughts came from. She found that a lot of her feelings came from the secrecy, unknown, and forced sexual exposure she had experienced. She started talking to a few of her roommates, friends, and her sister. They had discussions about things we processed through in therapy, their bodies, the male body, and sexual experiences they each had.

Emmie addressed the past exposure from her ex-boyfriend while in therapy. She was upset that she was introduced to the male body in such a horrific manner, that she had no choice, and that he sullied her experience of the male form. She decided that she no longer wanted to allow that exposure to control her and she started thinking of the male body differently. This took time and a great amount of effort but her opinion and thoughts about the male penis and testicles started to change. Emmie took into account aspects that she had not experienced with the exposure. She was able to think of the male penis as a beautiful part of the male body that possessed both an artistic form and strength. She started thinking about the penis as a symbol of male virility possessing a graceful power. Emmie's relationship with Luke helped her to see the male body in this way as Luke was a humanistic form of how she thought about the penis. He was sensitive, understanding, and loving, but he also had a strength about him that was comforting and reassuring.

With much of the sexual shame behind her, she started to see her sexual self as a single person. She noticed that she experienced desire from time to time. She sensed this desire when Luke would be sweet and loving with her. She also noticed her clitoris getting sensitive when she and Luke would kiss. She started looking forward to her sexual awakening and became proud that the core of her longed for more sexual touch. Of course she exercised restraint as she and Luke were just dating, but she relished in her body yearning for his touch.

For self-care Emmie started being kind and loving toward herself. She let go of telling herself that she should experience a certain level of sexual desire or arousal and instead relished in the desire and arousal that she did feel. This made it all the more present and enjoyable for her. She started to own her individualistic way of experiencing pleasure and reassured herself that her way was the right way. In this way, she eliminated expectations which allowed her to be present with herself and Luke. She started being loving and appreciative of her body and listened to it as it was telling her what felt good and to check-in. This happened by way of cupping her vulva and gently pressing. She included self-talk that shifted her narrative to "I'm grateful for this part of me and looking forward to expressing my sexual self. Now is not the time, but I hear you."

Along with these developments, Emmie was increasing her awareness of what was sexually exciting to her or arousing. She was more able to shift into a sexual excitatory mode, which was a brand-new world of fun for her. However, she was still single and wanted to adhere to her LDS values. So we worked on developing sexual inhibitions. She was really good at inhibiting her sexuality, since this had been the case for many years. However, the real trick lied in her inhibiting her sexuality minus shame, neglect, and self-hate. Emmie learned how to shift from her sexual world to her non-sexual world while still valuing her sexual self and sexual reality. This was amazing for Emmie because she could be in her non-sexual world but have quick access to her sexual self. In this way, she felt congruent.

The last thing that we worked on in therapy was eliminating expectation of how her sex life would be once she got married. This was a hard paradigm shift because she felt that the marital sex life would just be a continuation of her current sexual self and limited sexuality with her fiancé, whoever that would be. While elements of this are the case, typical LDS marital sex seems to be more of a new chapter rather than a continuation of a previous chapter. Emmie lived the remainder of her single life enjoying her sexual self and engagement with her sexual reality, while also knowing that she would start a new chapter of sexuality with her spouse and that all expectation would need to be let go of so as to eliminate comparison—which will kill pleasure.

If I could go back and work with Emmie for one last session, I'd have spent the time focusing on what Emmie's experience taught her versus what was taken away from her. As time has gone on I have thought about this and similar cases. All too often in our LDS culture that prizes sexual purity, we mourn what was lost in prior sexual relationships. I think there is a need for this since we as a culture and religion really value purity. However, we miss out on gaining value when we mourn to the extent that we discount how experience itself is of importance. In this way Emmie would reflect on the past with meaning and development instead of sadness.

I know that all of you want to know what happened to Emmie and Luke. They got married! They were able to eliminate comparison to their single life and enjoy their marital sexual intimacy for what it was. They created a positive sexual culture built on pleasure, love, and connection. They are still doing fabulous.

NEWLYWEDS

Y ou have waited for some time now to fall asleep together, call her wife or him husband, decorate your first home as a couple, and to have a sexual relationship. Perhaps you have been sexual alone, with someone else, or with each other before marriage. This may in fact be your first time touching another or allowing someone to touch you. Others may have had unwanted sexual activity in the form of rape, molestation, or exposure. This new stage is exciting for some and anxiety provoking for others. Truth be told the majority experience a wide range of emotions concerning this aspect of marriage. Even those that have been positively anticipating marriage with sex in mind can experience some anxiety since there is a lot of focus on sexuality for LDS members due to abstinence or attempts at abstinence. As an aside, hyper-focus on something that one is trying to neglect can at times produce the preoccupation with the thing one is trying to avoid.

Our religion is unique in a world that is becoming more and more amoral. I applaud all of you for attempting to be abstinent before marriage. Holding onto a part of yourself that is so primitive, beautiful, powerful, and godly deserves the highest accolades whether or not you were as successful as you would have liked. After sitting through hours and hours of sex therapy sessions with LDS clients, I can say that there are very few that have not had some type of sexual activity before marriage, either alone, with another, or with their spouse before marriage. I do not say this with a tone of acceptance. Rather, the reason that I mention this is to normalize what you may have experienced. Now that you are married, the utmost importance needs to be placed on that marriage. One of the most vital aspects of this holy relationship is your sexual relationship. It truly sets your relationship apart from any other relationship you have.

Some in this new stage of life have an easy time adjusting, and others struggle. Still others fall somewhere between having it easy and struggling. I remember having a conversation with a highly capable therapist and terrific person about her newlywed sexual relationship. She was well studied and read on the topic of sex and sexuality. Her parents raised her with a healthy view of sex and had regular conversations about this aspect of a marriage. She also grew up in a dramatically different culture than the LDS culture, so she had limited LDS cultural tones impacting her view of sex. There was much sex positive talk and messages in her culture. She fully embraced the idea that she and her new husband would be focusing on pleasure and neglecting performance-oriented sex.

To this newlywed couple's disappointment, she did not experience satisfaction. She in fact dealt with sexual pain for a good couple of months. My heart broke for her as she shared this experience. She was the most prepared LDS woman that I had ever spoken with. There was no physiological or pharmacological explanation for her pain and discomfort. Fortunately, she and her husband were tremendously adaptive and were able to find sexual enjoyment that varied from what they assumed other couples were doing. Soon she could have intercourse without pain or discomfort. The reason I'm telling you this story is to eliminate any self-punishment that you may be inflicting upon yourself. As my story illustrates, even the most well-prepared individual can struggle.

I have met with many clients that carry around shame for not being more sexually capable. They punish themselves for not being able to orgasm, experiencing desire as they were taught they should, or being able to enjoy sex. To those of you that fall into this category, I would say that self-punishment is not going to help anything. If you want things to change, refocus your efforts in other avenues. Get into a medical doctor, see a therapist, continue reading books, start talking to those you trust, and use the interventions within this book. Concerning intervention, you can begin by looking back at the chapter on SAAM and augmenting what you wrote for the systems within and the systems without. By now I'm confident that you are buying into this model. This will provide you with a roadmap for where to intervene. Remember that you alone are the only one responsible for your sexuality. You can get support from your spouse, but at the end of the day you are held accountable. It is not healthy to turn this over to your spouse or anyone else for that matter. If there are relational issues that are preventing your sexuality from flourishing then make every effort on your end to address said issues.

I have found the following to be the most helpful generally with newlyweds. If you are not already a standalone sexual person then get started. This doesn't mean that you necessarily need to start self-stimulating, as many would assume. Being a standalone sexual person means:

(1) Have a healthy relationship with your vagina and breasts or penis and testicles as well as those other parts of yourself that are sexual. How often have you held your penis and testicles and thought, "I'm grateful for you. I feel alive when I use you. I feel manly because of your shape, texture, size, form"? How often have you cradled your vagina or cupped your breast and felt the sexual capacity within your grasp? How often have you thought "I feel womanly, erotic, or aroused just by holding you firmly. My breasts move with sexual life as I walk, run, and move about my day. I'm proud of the unique and beautiful vulva. I love the sexual nature of my vulva that posses so much sexual potential. I like that I can squeeze my legs together and feel my clitoris awaken"? If you don't like your body then acceptance and loving yourself are just as important as having a relationship with your sexual anatomy.

(2) See your sexuality as an integrated element of your person and not something you conjure up or that is detached. Notice your sexual potential, feelings, and presence as you engage in your day. Examples include: in the shower, in front of the mirror, with a particular outfit on, as you lie on the bed and press gently into the mattress, as you sit in a chair and feel your genitalia against your legs and the seat.

(3) Sexualize yourself. Many women have a visceral reaction to this idea at first glance. Our society has taught us, rightfully so, that a lot of men sexualize women. In an attempt to combat this sexualization, women have de-sexualized themselves, especially among LDS members. They are uncomfortable with their breasts, how flattering clothing makes them look and appear to others, how brushing or rubbing against something might bring on arousal, how running brings breast movement that reminds of their womanly potential, and circumstances that make them feel sexually awake. Those that are not consensually sexualizing others

need to discontinue. However, when women de-sexualize themselves so that men do not sexualize them, women are surrendering their sexuality to a group of men instead of owning a God-given aspect of their person.

ELSA & DARREL: A CASE STUDY ABOUT CREATING A COUPLE SEXUAL CULTURE

Erase any expectation for how sex should be, and collaborate with your partner to create your own sexual culture. I promise you that what you two create can be better than anything that has been scripted as the norm or what others aim to achieve. You have your individual sexual likes, dislikes, fantasies, and vulnerabilities, and so does your spouse. Chances are that plenty of these are still unknown. What a beautiful river you two are sailing down. You can create a sexual culture that uniquely fits the two of you. This can also evolve over time just as people evolve. Enjoy the process of discovery, which will aid in you being present and not focused on performance, expectations, or the end that may or may not fit the two of you. As an example, I know of a woman and man that can have an orgasm very easily, no relation to each other. Elsa can have multiple orgasms just about whenever she wants. While Darrel has a refractory period, he can orgasm without even touching his penis. Needless to say, orgasm is very easy for him as well. Both describe orgasm as being an OK experience but true sexual intimacy that's connecting with their partner as being paramount to anything else—even the touted orgasm and multiple orgasm.

The bliss of being a newlywed can sometimes come crashing down as the couple is faced with unplanned financial obligations, increasing demands academically, a pregnancy, and the personality quarks that have been in the background while the couple was dating and not living each day together. These and other factors can contribute to the decline in marital satisfaction that a couple experiences. They were once able to solely focus on the relationship but soon life catches up to them. This is normal—even expected. It is a beautiful part of the river. Just as you are counseled to continue to date your spouse to keep the fire burning, you should also be aware that at times the sexual relationship takes work. After a long day at work and school, it can be difficult to think of having sex when the first thing that you want to do is dress in your sweats and watch a show. Sometimes newlyweds fall into a routine like this that only includes routine sex. Now there is nothing wrong with routine sex.

However, there is something wrong if all the sex you have is routine and all the sexual activity you engage in is intercourse. Begin early on in marriage by creating a dynamic that essentially says "We value our own sexual experiences and expression. We also value couple sexuality and expression, and we are going to act as such."

You cannot divorce yourself from your sexual experiences of the past. Everything that we experience has an impact on us. Narrowly stated, every sexual experience we have—be it getting a cat call, fantasizing about a girl in your class, or fondling a boyfriend—impacts our raft. If you have a sexual past, like most, then work on creating a narrative about those experience that will aid you and your spouse. As an aside, it is up to you to determine what to do with these experiences religiously. However, when it comes to your individual and couple sexuality, we need to incorporate these experiences so that they can have a healthy impact. For example, this may mean seeing past masturbation as a healthy and normative desire that you were often successful at avoiding. You can view your past experience as having a godly gift that you misused at times and now can enjoy a healthy form of sexual expression with your partner as the two of you are learning what makes couple sexuality different from individual sexuality and what makes it spiritually bonding. You are also working at enhancing positive sexuality. In this way, you are improving those things on the raft and riding the river.

MIDDLE AGE

Your kids are finally becoming more independent, you are finding more time in your schedule, and you have become less concerned about finances. Along with some of the aforementioned changes, you have more time and energy to analyze and work on your relationship. On the other hand, sometimes what comes with middle age is not what was planned. You may not experience more independence, time, and finances as was previously described. Middle age might be fraught with disappointment, increasing obligations, or medical challenges. These are but a few hallmarks for couples of middle age. At this stage of life, couples look to improve their relationship either due to their increased freedom or out of defiance for the way that things have been. Some of you are looking for ways to augment the satisfying relationship you already have. Others are looking for ways to get the relationship back to where it was in years past. Still many others are hoping to gain a sexual relationship that they never had with their spouse. There are some of you that are trying to figure out if it is worth it to stay married now that the kids are mostly raised. I would assume that one of these scenarios fits you.

This stage of marriage can often have an additional relational context for LDS couples. Middle age for LDS couples often looks relationally different than it does for non-LDS couples for a few reasons. A lot of self-sacrifice takes place in LDS marriages for the good of the family or out of the seriousness given to marriage or covenants made between God and the couple. It is very common for a couple to struggle through marriage so that they can raise their children in a covenant marriage or for one of both partners to stay married due to the seriousness they give to their marriage and covenants. If this is you, I applaud your devotion and commitment to God and your family. Because of this you may have looked past attachment injuries, relational red flags, or other things that would have caused a couple not as concerned with a covenant marriage to separate or divorce long before. That's not to say that divorce doesn't have a place and it's not my place to say who should or shouldn't get divorced.

Despite what river you find yourself floating down, this can be a very fun transition stage. If you can hearken your thoughts back to the early stages of dating, you will find some similarities to this state of your relationship. You have probably been asking yourself "where do we begin?" A lot has happened since you have been able to stay out all night and not worry about the kids, get lost on a meandering walk, or take a spur-of-the-moment road trip. One or both partners may wonder if they still have the spark in their relationship, if their spouse will still choose them, or if the love is still in the marriage. In a way, this transition state is very similar to the early part of dating where many similar questions existed. Such questions included wondering if you two had that special thing to make a life together work, if the other person will continue to choose to be with you, or whether or not they love you. It is upon this contextual aspect that I urge you to begin cultivating a spirit of hope and excitement where passion can reside.

If the two of you are unable to accept—not agree with, but accept—past hurts and let go of resentments then I counsel you to meet with a marital therapist and begin resolving these injuries so that you can enjoy your relationship long into old age. If you are ruminating on past events, cannot see your partner for more than these injuries, or do not allow yourself to trust them then I'd say that therapy would be a good option for you two. If you are able to let go of resentments, start trusting, and be vulnerable with your spouse then you are well on your way to enjoying a more fulfilling sex life.

Robert Sternberg developed what he called the "Triangular Theory of Love."[1] There are three main components that this theory rests upon. These components are at the points of the triangle and are passion, commitment, and intimacy. These three are requisite for the consummate love, which is the holy grail of love that we all seek. Consummate love is something we should be ever striving for, as it is not as simple as arriving and kicking your feet up. I feel this is significantly relevant for middle-age LDS couples because many find themselves or their partners possessing one or two points on the triangle and feeling this to be the case for years in their marriage. For the large majority of you, your love will possess commitment, commitment and intimacy (companionate), or commitment and passion (fatuous) (Sternberg, pg. 119–135).

We all know of someone with a commitment-only relationship. They usually describe themselves as living parallel lives with their spouse or as roommates. Sternberg describes this as empty love. The couple doesn't usually enjoy spending time together or feel passion, romance, or desire for their spouse. Sex may be described by these couples as empty, purely biological, hollow, or missing connection. Unfortunately, one or both partners can feel sexually used by their spouse.

Commitment and intimacy couples describe themselves as being married to their best friend. Sound familiar? This is a very common kind of marriage. They like spending time together and have common interests. They can depend on their partner and have no fears of them leaving. The sex life of these couples may feel sterile, lacking passion, dull, formal, too scripted or wholesome, or perhaps borderline inappropriate. Because of this, these couples often ironically feel that their sex life is the only place they can't be vulnerable or feel connection.

Commitment and passion couples describe their relationship as a rollercoaster and can feel as if they don't really know each other. Sometimes they can't stand to be around each other, and other times they are stuck together like glue. They frequently have a difficult time getting along, so fighting and long nights of drama are commonplace in these relationships. These couples are typically the ones having make-up sex or hate sex. Their sexual relationship is as volatile as the rest of their relationship. They may feel that sex can lack respect, spirit, compassion, connection, or true intimacy.

There is a chance that you find yourself in a passion and intimacy relationship, also known as infatuation. If you do then there is a possibility that you are in a new relationship since these relationships are void of commitment, will not last that long, or are fraught with insecurity and uncertainty. These sexual relationships can look similar to the sexual relationships of couples with only commitment and passion. Partners in these relationships can have a very difficult time wanting to be vulnerable with their spouse, which can have a disastrous effect on the couple's sex life and overall relationship.

Now that you know where the two of you are in the Triangular Theory of Love, we can create a roadmap toward consummate love and relationship. Esther Perel highlights the difficulty that many monogamous couples face concerning their sexual relationship.[2] She posits that intimacy and passion work against each other in a sense. According to Perel, intimacy includes predictability, safety, comfort, knowing, and nothing left to the imagination. Intimacy comes in having no gap in a relationship or space between partners. Only then is a partner able to feel intimacy—and therefore security—in their relationship. Paradoxically, passion comes from a place of uncertainty, unpredictability, unexpected, questioning, not knowing, and guessing. Passion comes from the process of closing the gap between the two individuals.

Perel says that seeing your partner at a distance doing what they are really good at is an example of having this space to close.[3] Two weeks ago, my wife was teaching Relief Society. I was given the responsibility from our Bishopric to ensure that things discussed in the Teacher Council Meetings were being translated into the classroom. So I decided that I'd attend my wife's lesson. Now I know that my wife is an excellent teacher. However, as I sat there watching her do something that she is very good at, I experienced the passion component that Perel discusses. In a way, I saw my wife in a similar way to when we were dating. She used to be the music chorister in her singles ward. I would attend her ward most Sundays when we were getting pretty serious. I still remember looking up at her thinking, "She's beautiful and so talented. I hope that she'll really marry me. I want to really know her even more than I do now. I want to know what it's like to spend a life with her." I wanted to close the space between us and eliminate the unknown. It is in that space that our passion flourished. As you fast forward many years later I was thinking some of the same things about my wife while I witnessed her beauty and talent teaching Relief Society.

If one partner is a stay-at-home parent or does not work, it becomes increasingly difficult for their spouse to see this person from afar. It will be vital that this partner is supported in having things in their life that foster growth, adventure, change, or differentiation. While the other spouse is out doing, accomplishing, learning, seeing things, and having experiences, the other may have a routine life. It is far easier to look at the spouse outside of the home with eyes of passion.

Keep in mind that it is difficult to be seen from afar and admired when you have no hobbies, have no interests, or do nothing but work or stay at home. Again, this can be particularly difficult for the stay-at-home parent. It is hard to see your partner from afar when they are always home. Thus, the need to support their hobbies and interests outside of family life is paramount.

In this stage of your relationship, couples complain that the space between—kids, career, callings, and so on—has made it difficult for the couple to feel in tandem as they once did at the onset of their relationship. One can either look at this with upset and frustration about the work that needs to be put back into the relationship or a couple can see that their relationship is ripe with the seeds of passion. There is much gap between partners in this stage of life, and therefore passion can easily be fostered as the couple gets to know each other again. As stated before, a lot has taken place and there has been much change over the years of marriage and family life. Not everything will be a refresher when you truly get to know each other again. I daresay that many things will be new including aspects of sexuality. In this space where passion can grow, you will find passion spilling over into the sexual relationship. Enjoy discovering, wondering, not knowing. Relish in the fact that your relationship is ripe with the seeds of passion all ready for the taking. Keep in mind that passion grew in yesteryears out of time you and your partner placed into getting to know each other and spending time with each other. In this manner, it is time to really date your spouse. Date as you did when your relationships first started to grow, which is probably dramatically different from how you have been dating. You will need to put more into this aspect of your relationship if your marriage has been void of the intimacy point on the triangle.

ACTIVITY

In the space below, write down how you dated your spouse before marriage. What time and effort went into thinking about him or her, preparing for a date, being attentive during dinner, not judging him or her, seeing the beauty in him or her, and so on?

_____

_____

_____

_____

_____

_____

_____

Now that you can remember how you used to date one another, think of how you would like to date your spouse. What ways are you willing to change how you date your spouse? Only you are responsible for the effort that you put into your relationship. Now is the time to let go of those things that have held you back. Write down the roadblocks to vulnerability and action steps to change.

_____

_____

_____

_____

_____

_____

_____

JAMIE & ADAM: A CASE STUDY ABOUT PASSION

Jamie and Adam had created a wonderful life together. They had four children, a beautiful house, good friends, and an active family and Church life. Two of the children were out of the house—one married and the other on a mission. The two youngest were still finishing up high school.

The couple appeared to have the ideal life to any onlooker. They even had the therapist fooled for some time because they were very agreeable, kind, communicative, and loving toward each other in therapy. This all began to break down a few months into treatment as the same ongoing fight began to manifest. Both partners vocalized their dismay at the perpetual state of their marriage. There was love, respect, loyalty, but nothing that could be termed an active or enjoyable sex life. Sure, the couple had a sexual relationship from time to time. Jamie complained that she just "helped him out" or agreed to have sex every once in a while. Adam despised the patterns in their sexual relationship almost as much as Jamie. He was upset at the lack of concern or desire that Jamie had for sex and for him for that matter. However, they didn't know what to do in order to bring about a change. They had been at this for the last fifteen years of their twenty-six-year marriage, and the fight seemed as fresh as the day it first began.

Over the next few months, Jamie and Adam were able to state their frustration in a loving but honest way. Each spouse heard and validated the other without having to agree. Both partners said that this helped them to feel heard and known by the other. The next stages of therapy helped Jamie and Adam to see that this was a normal issue to have considering career, family life, and other obligations and stressors. We then turned our attention to the positive aspects of the couple's relationship. They were able to have strong loyalty for the last twenty-six years. The couple was also able to hold onto a genuine respect, kindness, compassion, and liking of each other. Jamie and Adam had a relationship strong with commitment and intimacy. However, they were lacking passion to keep their love vibrant and alive.

The next stage of change for Jamie and Adam was to embark on a quest to embrace and cultivate passion. Over the years they had lost a sense of this in all the hubbub of raising kids, buying and selling homes, career, finances, family, and callings. The couple really buckled down and had to each respectively say that their sex life mattered and that they were not going to put it last on the list anymore. They soon found that as they made a space to date each other, once again as they used to, their passion for each other and desire to really get to know each other and be known by the other increased dramatically. Their sex life followed suit.

Jamie started to look forward to the time during the week that Adam would make a surprise visit home, and the two of them would flirt, touch, talk, and even have sex in the kitchen. Adam started bringing Jamie along with him on business trips where he would have some cute date planned unique for that city. Both Jamie and Adam started really seeing each other amidst the busy lives that they created. This included lying down talking, touching, and looking eye-to-eye with each other like they did when they were dating all those years ago. They would even put on music and just lay there together—sometimes naked and other times just holding hands or embracing. Even more, they made these busy lives about their relationship and not about career, the house, activities, and so on. Jamie and Adam illustrate how a couple can lose sight of a consummate love and relationship. Oftentimes it is felt that commitment alone, commitment and intimacy, or commitment and passion are enough. If we are genuinely striving for a godly type of love and covenant marriage with our spouse, are we really fooling ourselves in leaving off one of these points on the triangle?

❧ Notes ❧

1. Robert J. Sternberg, "A Triangular Theory of Love," *Psychological Review* 93, no. 2 (1986): 119–35.
2. Esther Perel, "The Secret to Desire in a Long-Term Relationship," filmed February 2013 in New York, NY, TED video, 19:03, https://www.ted.com/talks/esther_perel_the_secret_to_desire_in_a_long_term_relationship/.
3. See Perel.

EMPTY NESTERS

At the empty nester stage, there can be a loss of self felt by one or both partners. Decades have been spent raising children, providing safety, giving financial support, cultivating a loving home, instilling life skills, teaching values, and cherishing moments with your children. In what may appear to be one moment, this and much more is gone. You and your spouse are left feeling as though a part of you—perhaps the largest part of you—has walked out the door along with these children.

These feelings are common to feel by loving and amazing parents. At this stage of life, you and your partner are left wondering what to do. You probably have planned to make trips out to see the kids and grandkids, move to be closer once retirement begins, help raise the grandchildren close by, or donate more time to callings or volunteer work.

CATHERINE & LEE: A CASE STUDY ABOUT SENSE OF SELF

Catherine and Lee experienced something very similar to this. They had moved their last daughter to college three years prior to meeting in therapy. They had raised five children and done the best they could at being parents and grandparents. Since becoming empty nesters, they had made many visits to see the children living farther away. Lee had taken a few of the grandchildren fishing and camping whenever his work and other obligations would allow. Catherine was always available to babysit for her daughters close to home.

When Catherine finally brought Lee into therapy, she and I had already been meeting for the last four months. Catherine originally came into therapy because a good friend referred her to meet with me. Her problem was adjusting to the transition of this stage of life and feeling lost. After feeling comfortable in therapy, she divulged that she was really discontent with her sexual relationship and had hoped that she and Lee could find sexual fulfillment even though they were "past their prime." It hadn't been since they were newlyweds that she felt like herself sexually, and she longed for this again. After a little coaxing, Catherine convinced Lee that therapy wouldn't be all that bad.

The main focus of treatment for Catherine and Lee was to help them to gain a sense of self outside of all the roles and responsibilities that they were shrouded in. Lee had been a husband, father, provider, grandfather, scoutmaster, high council member, protector, and many other roles over the years since he and Catherine got married. Catherine had been an employee, mother, wife, nursery leader, homemaker, relief society counselor, visiting teacher, businesswoman, and grandmother.

Catherine and Lee were taught that sometimes our sense of self, or who we are, gets lost in all the roles and responsibilities that we take on throughout life. Our sense of self is paramount in cultivating sexual desire. If we lose self in our roles then we can easily lose sexual desire. Interestingly, from a young age, our self—or who we are—is nurtured. Parents, neighbors, friends, and many others unwittingly do this. They expose us to activities, culture, events, and other things that they feel might help us gain a sense of who we are. We are asked how we enjoy dance, clothing, scouts, literature, music, and academics. High school in large part is about gaining our identity or sense of self. Whenever you had the opportunity to find yourself you may cite this period of life as one where you felt most alive.

Almost as soon as we gain our self of identity, we are asked to lose it. We are bombarded by questions about what we'll study in college, what our career will be, if we're going to get married, or if we'll have children, and other roles or responsibilities begin to be placed upon our heads. As we take more of these on, we have a tendency to lose identify or self. We give up dance to finish college on time. We stop playing board games or basketball so that we can get a job promotion. In the blink of an eye our identity can be surrendered—and along with it, passion and sexual desire. This is essentially what happened with Catherine and Lee.

Lee knew that he needed to act soon or else he would live out his years squandering his sexuality. He took off a whole week to go camping and fishing and vowed to take mini trips more frequently. He in fact kept his vow and went on many mini trips. Lee also began tinkering around in the garage under the hood of his old 1967 Mustang that he had held onto for many years. Catherine hit the library and lost herself in bubble bath and book after book. Catherine also found a group of women in her community that played cards. The couple took up line dancing and traveling to Southern Utah for the outdoor theater. These were but a few of the ways that they began to find themselves as individuals and a couple again.

Finding one's identity again is no easy task. I have worked with lots of people that just take up another role, as this has been their pattern over the life-course. Find the things in life that energize you, get your heart racing, you can't stop thinking about, you lose track of time doing, or make you feel alive. For Catherine, she gets lost in books and a good storyline. She can spend hours in a library or bookstore perusing books. The time flies when she is playing cards and laughing with friends. Lee loves to figure out how things work and to make things out in his shop. He will now wake up early on the weekend to spend another hour or two under the hood of his car listening to music. The two found passion for life, which they could bring back to their relationship. After a day of Lee working on his car and Catherine being out with her friends, the two of them enjoy coming back together to talk about their interests. These interests and passions made them all the more desirable to their spouse and they haven't been able to keep their hands off each other ever since.

In the space below, write down when you found your identity and what was included in your sense of self. Then write down what you need to do in order to begin to find this again and action steps. Begin each morning by reviewing through meditation.

OLD AGE

O ne of my favorite studies asked individuals in old age, who described feeling sexual satisfaction across their lifespan, "What factors made it so that you were sexually satisfied throughout your life?" Many different words or sentences were used to describe this but the one word that sums up the most cited factor is *adaptability*. There are many circumstances that take place across an individual's lifespan that can impact their sexuality. These include illness, injury, medication, partner characteristics, loss, trauma, aging, familial factors, death, depression, job loss, financial strains, and so on. Each of us can count on many factors such as these impacting our sexuality, especially as we live into old age. I know that I have discussed being adaptive early on in this book. However, as I contemplated the most relevant sexual factor to discuss in old age, my thoughts continued to turn to the need to adapt or be flexible.

As SAAM states, we have little control over the river—life—but still limited control over our raft—individual sexuality. At some point, we are going to need to accept that our sexuality requires flexibility in order to optimize our sexual experience and satisfaction. In early life, our need to be flexible might be at a minimum if non-existent. We may have planned to marry a spouse that has the same sex drive, interests, and prioritization as us. You may have in fact found this—though rare—sexual equal. As life unfolds, one spouse might become mired down in depression or early menopause, repressed sexual abuse may unfold, or the strains and obligations of parenthood and life may carry away their sexuality, bashing their raft against the rocks and sandbars. Your individual and couple sexuality may have taken a hit at middle age. The two of you may have bound your rafts together from time to time and borrowed or leaned on each other's sexuality to get through turbulent waters only to free the other's raft to continue to sail on.

In old age, the river can rage again. Common sexual impacts come by way of medication, illness, aging, depression, anxiety, change, loss, isolation, fear, uncertainty, and financial concerns. The need to adapt to the ever-changing river is paramount. As you look around, you may notice that the landscape of your river looks foreign to the river you and your partner used to navigate. You used to work around children's sleeping schedules, multiple callings, or career obligations to ensure that you two didn't lose an essential and defining characteristic of your selves, your sexuality. Perhaps sexual functioning didn't have much variation or change as is the landscape you find yourself currently navigating. Before, keeping your sex life alive meant making sure to prioritize or be creative in when or how long you could be intimate. You may have found that a morning sexual encounter in the bathroom was sometimes the only way to make sure you were connecting and feeling sexually fulfilled. Similarly, the two of you may have made a habit out of going to a hotel from time to time so that you didn't feel rushed sexually, or you were sexual when the kids left for school.

I want you to keep the aforementioned in mind because you will need that flexibility in old age. If the above doesn't fit you, then you will need to learn to be adaptive in order to achieve the sexual satisfaction that you seek. In my practice, I have found that sexual flexibility is often more of a concern for those of older age. The older age cohort has almost always been more sexually conservative than the younger age cohorts, as the world becomes more sexually permissive and sexually transparent across time. Television programs, for example, are an illustration of this. I used to sit up at night and watch old reruns of shows like *I Love Lucy* with my sister. None of the couples in this show slept in the same bed. They always had two twin beds sitting apart from each other. Nowadays the sexual expression included in television programs can make even the most progressive person blush in the right company.

FRIEDA & GEORGE: A CASE
STUDY ABOUT ADAPTABILITY

A while back, I met with Frieda and George, who found me in hope of improving or regaining their sex life. George had undergone invasive prostate cancer surgery. They were both in old age and had multiple medications they used. Frieda was losing her memory slowly and feared the time when it would turn into full-blown dementia. Despite these and other struggles the couple was having, they had always valued their sexual relationship and were not willing to live out their rest of their years without being sexually intimate. The couple had already lost two years since George's surgery without being sexual.

When asked why the couple did not continue sexual intimacy after the doctors had given the green light for sex subsequent to cancer treatment, Frieda said that George couldn't have sex and so they didn't have any other option. After many questions, George finally blurted out, "I can't get an erection and the medication that Doc gave me doesn't work, so we just can't have sex." Frieda and George had been sexually active almost every week, and sometimes multiple times weekly, during their marriage. They had always had intercourse and never varied from this type of sexual activity.

The next several sessions were spent asking about their feelings concerning other sexual activity. Much of this other sexual activity, such as oral sex and manual intercourse, were only things they knew vaguely about, and they didn't ever talk to each other about adding these elements to their sex life. Therapy included psycho-education and processing feelings and opinions from the couple. Eventually, Frieda had started to think about oral sex and how it might feel. She longed to feel close to George and have sexual expression again. This new desire for oral sex began to grow in her, as she had never experienced such an encounter. She brought this up in one of the sessions. George was excited to hear that Frieda had thought about this and the couple had a dialogue about it as an activity outside of therapy. The couple battled the fact that George wouldn't be able to progress to intercourse due to George's erectile dysfunction. Many more sessions were spent educating the couple about varied sexual expression and that there should be no end goal or pursuit other than pleasure. Having such hinders a couple's experience. Frieda and George were a case in point.

With time, the couple learned to adapt to the physical, mental, and other constraints on their lives. Frieda vocalized feeling more herself sexually than ever before and enjoying her sexual expression more than just through intercourse. George missed having intercourse because this was his ideal form of expression. He was grateful for having gone through cancer treatment however, as he would never have been able to satisfy Frieda in the way that she was now satisfied. Frieda and George found a few ways to have intercourse and enjoyed the times this was possible, but they didn't put it on a pedestal over the other encounters they had. George soon found further sexual satisfaction by form of manual and oral sex as well as novelty items that he had long before wanted to use with Frieda but feared discussing. The couple essentially mourned losses and adapted. They cherished sexual stages of their lives or points on the river and were now finding the joy in the current state of their river.

REMARRIAGE

emarriage is a new exciting frontier for you to be rafting down. Whether you have been sailing for months, years, or decades alone, your river has finally converged with the river of another, and you look forward to what this new sexual journey beholds for the two of you. Just like the joining of two rivers may mean sometimes turbulent waters upfront as they forge a path together, so too does merging your sex life with a new spouse. You have been married once or more before, and the sexual relationship with your former partner or partners will probably be different from this new relationship.

The way that you and your spouse set up your sexual relationship at the onset will set the tone for the future years. The same can be said for first-time marriages. The difference between a first marriage in your younger years and this remarriage are the increased responsibilities and obligations that you have assumed as you have grown, matured, and engaged with life. A young newlywed couple, for instance may only have financial, work, and academic obligations outside of the relationship. This is a lot for anyone to take on and I by no means am saying that it's easy. However, a remarriage may mean the before mentioned along with blending and raising children, moving, selling a house, changing jobs, and past attachment injuries from your former marriage.

The couple's sex life can easily become lost in the hustle and bustle of combining lives and families and trying to make a remarriage work with past attachment injuries. Along with making the sexual relationship a priority, the main impact on the couple's sexuality is attachment injuries. These are what I want to focus my main comments on in this section.

Straight from the womb, an infant is setup to form attachments with parents. Attachments are what make children feel safe and secure in the world and are essential to growth and development. Attachments do not stop after childhood or teenage years. Attachments are foundational and informative all throughout the lifespan. Attachments are just as crucial in survival for human beings as physical safety. Our early attachments inform our future attachments. When one grows up feeling insecurely attached, this individual will most likely struggle with romantic attachments. Subsequent consequences are sexual challenges. The result may look like neediness or distancing within the relationship. Not only do our early attachments impact our future attachments, but also our romantic relationships can alter our safety and security or attachment.

When we have experienced an attachment injury from a significant other or former spouse, that injury teaches us something about people. At its core, it perhaps teaches us that we can't rely on others. When we don't feel safe with others, people tend to be needy or avoid closeness. Either of these two processes helps one to feel safe and secure. Neither is healthy, but what we are up against is a more primitive need at the center of all of us.

The good news is that just as an unhealthy relationship can create an insecure attachment for each of us, a healthy relationship can aid in helping us form secure attachments to others. Attachment injuries incurred from former spouses are sure to have impacted safety felt in your new relationship. An awareness of this and direction can make all the difference in building a healthy sexual relationship into a remarriage.

Essentially what anyone needs that finds themselves with an insecure attachment is a secure base and a safe haven in significant attachment figures.[1] These figures can be siblings, parents, friends, God, and spouse, to name a few. A secure base means that one feels loved, special, compassion, cared for, and safe to go out into the scary world. A safe haven means that one feels they can go to this person for refuge from the storm of life and get love, compassion, understanding, care, and safety. Through time, one should start to feel more secure in his or her attachments. I recommend reading Sue Johnson's book *Hold Me Tight*[2] and going to marriage counseling if you find yourself significantly struggling in this regard. I have found that the aspect of one's river that is most crucial to developing or destroying a sexual relationship in remarriages is the couple relationship and safety felt therein.

MELANIE & CHIP: A CASE STUDY ABOUT BUILDING ATTACHMENT

Melanie and Chip were a remarried couple trying to blend their lives together. Melanie had a child from a previous relationship and Chip had two from two past relationships. The couple started coming to therapy to work on Melanie's inability to orgasm with Chip. Neither of them were satisfied with their sex life even outside of her inability to orgasm. They complained that it felt empty and strictly physical. Melanie had experienced perpetual emotional abuse from her former spouse. Chip was trying to be supportive and loving, but he was at a loss for what to do to help her heal and to improve their sex lives.

As time went on, Melanie divulged that she could orgasm on her own very easily but was unable to experience this with Chip. Chip was upset to hear this, since he felt that he was a good husband. With time, Chip was able to be empathic with Melanie as she worked through her attachment injuries from her past relationship. Chip was incorporated into therapy as a secure attachment figure that could empathize, validate, comfort, support, be a sounding board, and provide safety and security for Melanie. Melanie expressed feeling that she felt heard, understood, known, and truly seen by Chip. Chip was not only able to provide this in therapy, but also outside of the therapy room. Melanie was accumulating new emotional experiences that were disconfirming her old-held beliefs that others were not safe. Chip was a pillar of safety and security for her. Melanie found herself talking to Chip and crying on his shoulder with disappointments in parenting and feeling unfulfilled in certain aspects of life. In this way, she could come to him as a safe haven from the storm of life. Melanie also found herself feeling the warmth of security from being seen and understood by Chip as he left for work each morning and as she embarked on her day. Melanie in this sense truly found a secure base in Chip in which she could springboard off of into the world.

At this point in therapy, Melanie and Chip were ready to bring what they had learned into the bedroom. Activities that would capitalize on Melanie's relational safety were given, and the couple began having low pressure and pleasure-focused sexual activities to engage in between therapy sessions. Melanie felt as though she could truly show up and be seen with Chip during sex. She allowed herself to be vulnerable and be known during sex as she never had before. In past encounters, Melanie would be physically present but emotionally disengaged as a form of defense. She was only able to move past this by first being vulnerable and feeling safe and secure with Chip outside of sex. She knew that he was there for her and that his love was not contingent or movable. With time, Melanie showed Chip how she liked to be touched and pleasured. She incorporated him into her self-touch and was able to kick out insecure thoughts because she knew Chip was safe. Chip took direction from Melanie and the two of them incorporated pleasure into their sexual encounters by mutually touching Melanie. With time, Melanie would rub against his hand and Chip could bring her to orgasm. A few months later and with a little more direction from therapy, Melanie was able to orgasm during intercourse. What had really held this couple up was the lack of emotional engagement in their sexual relationship. Melanie and Chip took the time to place emotional presence into their overall relationship and then their sexual relationship by addressing attachment injuries from Melanie's past relationship.

❧ NOTES ❧

1. Sue Johnson, "Attachment and the Dance of Sex: Integrating Couple and Sex Therapy," DrSueJohnson.com, accessed Oct. 24, 2017, http://www.drsuejohnson .com/attachment-sex/attachment-and-the-dance-of-sex-integrating-couple-and -sex-therapy/.
2. See Sue Johnson, *Hold Me Tight: Seven Conversations for a Lifetime of Love* (New York: Little, Brown, 2008).

MAINTAINING a HEALTHY SEX LIFE: PATHWAYS to SEXUAL PLEASURE

P athways to sexual pleasure mean the way in which one gets from their normal everyday life to a place of sexual desire. It is a little easier for a stereotypical man to find these pathways as they are echoed through media and just about anywhere you look. There are plenty of women that also find pathways to sexual pleasure in a way that is more stereotypical to men. However, these very clear pathways such as sexual fantasy, sexual touch, strip tease, erotic discussion, etc. don't fit everyone. Men included.

Many men look to sex as a way to re-engage their resting brains. In fact, many men and some women teach themselves to look to sex when they are bored, lonely, or restless. The person more focused on sex during these idle times is primed and poised for sexual activity. This is neither good nor bad. It becomes problematic only when it is the only avenue to meet boredom, connection, lowliness, stress, etc.

Dissimilarly, many women have a more difficult time calming down their brains and resting so that sexual activity is desirable. Female brains do not get much of a rest and instead are thinking of such things as relationships, their to-do list, or other events that occurred during the day. It is because of this that some women have a difficult time switching the sex switch on. It is also because of this that some men seem to have their on switch always switched on. Both of these states can become detrimental to the overall relationship.

Whether you fit this neuroscience research or not, it is important for you to figure out if your normal idle state is sex conscious or sex aloof. If it's sex conscious, then it'll be important for you to enhance other aspects of your marital relationship so that your partner doesn't feel used, undervalued, or unimportant. This means that the sex-conscious person needs to make a concerted effort to be more communicative, thoughtful, emotionally engaged, and relationally focused. Below you will find some activities that can help one's partner to feel more sexual pleasure since the focus is not solely on sex. By focusing on other aspects of the relationship, the less sex-conscious person will find more pleasure when engaged in sexual activity.

Sex-aloof spouses will need to make a concerted effort to be more sexually aware. They will need to look for pathways that foster sexual desire and arousal. This may mean letting go of their busy brain at times and allowing themselves to completely relax. This can be difficult since their idle is using a lot more brainpower to think of other things than that of their partner's. These people need less active brain time so that they can enjoy the thought of re-engaging the brain through such activities as sex. I have included some couple activities that will help this spouse find pathways to sexual pleasure when also applying true relaxation and mindfulness that is sex positive.

Here I have included some pathways to sexual pleasure that often work for both sexes. I'm not sure how the world started prioritizing ways of connecting, feeling loved, or communicating emotions, but I want to set the record straight. There are many ways that individuals connect to each other. The general worldly themes appear to be verbally promoting and physically disparaging. This can be hard if you are one of few words or have a hard time talking about feelings. That doesn't mean that you have a free pass, but it does mean that just as much importance needs to be placed in the physical, sexual, thoughtful, or other ways that one communicates to their spouse. These pathway activities include tracing each other's bodies, holding and talking, holding and feeling, listening to breath, getting to know each other's body, hand caress, talking to the other's heart, whisper pleasure, simulating pleasure, and pillow talk. All of these activities can be done naked, partially clothed, or clothed. I suggest doing each. Each activity can be erotic, sensual, or both.

Pathways to Sexual Pleasure Activities

Tracing each other's bodies can be a way that couples feel close, disconnect from the world, and find pathways to pleasure. Partners takes their turn and they trace the other's naked body. The one being traced focuses on the touch and connection and pushes out the world. Positively anticipating the next touch and focusing on physical touch is the name of the game. Trace each other's faces as well. End with a full body caress. If you go through the motions or are not being present then you will not find a pathway to pleasure.

The focus of holding and talking is not to get your partner to have sex with you, but to feel connected, heard, and understood. Hold your partner in a chair, tub, or couch. It may sound simple but think about the last time that you two tuned your busy lives out and just talked and listened to each other without feeling time constraints. Try to focus on things other than your typical daily conversations of the kids, work, or other obligations. Talk about the two of you, what you hope for your relationship, or what you two have overcome together.

Holding and feeling requires no words but consists of being present with one another. You are trying to feel close without talking and just feeling. Take turns being held by the other spouse. The spouse holding you will feel your body in ways that are connecting and relationally healing. This may mean some sexual touch, but most likely the focus will be sensual. Focus not on what you want, but on how your partner will feel closer to you. This isn't a massage. It's connection through touch.

Listening to breath can be done by laying your head on your partner's chest or having them breathe near your ear. The purpose of this activity is to feel close and connected to your spouse by tuning into his or her breath, which is literally a manifestation of your partner's life, presence, and expression. Connect to this and help your partner feel heard in his or her existence. In this way, you are saying that "you matter more than all the other things rattling around in my head or that acknowledging your existence matters more than just sex." The partner being listened to can vary his or her breath by making it deep or shallow for example.

In the activity, getting to know each other's bodies is the purpose; forget yourself and help your partner's presence be known. This can feel very erotic as your partner can tell the difference from selfish touch to selfless touch. Explore the various and individualist ways that your partner might feel known by you through touch. Each body part might want to be known in a different way than the last body part.

The hand caress is a more simplistic version of the activity. Your full attention is on your partner feeling connected through the hand to hand contact. Think back to your days of dating when nothing else in the world existed outside of him or her touching your hand. This activity can be done in a multiplicity of venues and should be to provide a pathway to sexual pleasure in the moment, later that day, or at a different time in the week.

Talking to your partner's heart is a very vulnerable experience when done correctly. It can be done by resting your head on your partner's heart, softly kissing and looking at their heart, or resting your forehead against your partner's forehead. You then lower your defenses and talk. You can vocalize relational fears you have, reasons why you put up walls, or things you appreciate or look forward to with your spouse for example. You can also whisper this to your partner's ear. Some people find that it's easier to lower one's defenses this way. Do not make this an attack, but instead a vulnerable expression of feeling.

Whisper pleasure is done through erotically whispering what it feels like as your pleasure builds and fades away. Pleasure in its best form doesn't always end in orgasm and neither does your expression need to end in orgasm. There is no expectation that this activity will need to end in intercourse or more than just this experience together.

Simulate pleasure is done through you acting out a pleasurable sexual experience. This can be one that has happened or one that you hope to have happen. Be creative in how you act this act. Remember that you are acting, so acting out intercourse doesn't mean that you have intercourse. It may mean that you straddle your partner and act out what would feel good. Simulating pleasure may mean acting out pleasure while you sensually touch your partner and mimic your arousal. Exaggerate, have fun, be flirty— maybe even go outside your box.

To do pillow talk, you and your partner take turns coming up with sexual fantasies. These don't have to be things you are committing to engage in. They can be activities you have done, things you have thought about, or just things that are fun and flirty to talk about. Remember that all of these activities are based on finding pathways that lead to sexual pleasure in your relationship. They are avenues for you or your partner to take that will help lead you to a more satisfying sex life—a sex life that needs variability, broader focus than just intercourse, and connection to your spouse.

In the space below, write down some physical, sexual, and emotional ways that you and your spouse find pathways to sexual pleasure. Ensure that you have well-rounded pathways since your partner may enjoy a variety unfamiliar or dissimilar to your own.

_____

_____

_____

_____

_____

_____

Collectively describe in the space below new pathways that you would like to engage in over the coming week, month, and year. Include steps to achieve this. Remember that pathways to sexual pleasure do not always mean pathways to intercourse.

_____

_____

_____

_____

_____

_____

SHIFTING: OUR CULTURAL NARRATIVE

The longer I have engaged in the world of sex therapy with the LDS population, the more I see a paradigm shift needed. I feel as though I'm not the only one that desires an altered view of how we as a collective body think about sexuality and our role as LDS members in terms of sexuality. Over the last year I have felt as though there is a change in the air.

Through discussions in teaching, with clients, and speaking to fellow members of the LDS faith I am experiencing something phenomenal. There exists intolerance for our past collective narrative for sexuality in the LDS culture and a desire for change. Some of the old collective view included such thoughts as "Only certain sexual acts are considered normal" and "Spiritual women don't think about sex or crave sex" and "I can't enjoy how sex feels without it being strictly holy and reverenced" and "LDS members are reserved sexually." These are but a few of the ideas that have added to our collective narrative about LDS sexuality. While there are those that did not feel this way, the large majority of our culture experienced feeling, thinking, and struggling with such impressions. I know that the cultural and individual intent had always been to follow God's commandments so that we could live with Him again. It appears that many of our faith are seeing that these before mentioned ideas weren't doctrine. I've come across no Church doctrine (in talks and the like) that imposes such restrictions. Even more, there is a collective shift on foot that says we can still follow God's commandments and live with Him if we don't fit these old cultural beliefs about sexuality. It is truly an exciting time to be LDS! Let's start shifting.

The new cultural narrative we are *shifting* to is very sex positive. It is sexuality promoting and honoring. Some of the new ideas that are included in our new narrative are "Sex needs to be discussed" and "Expressing oneself sexually is normal" and "Sexual touch and interaction feels good and there is nothing wrong with that" and "We are having ongoing conversations with our children about sexuality as they grow" and "I'm normal for liking this different position, touch, or expression" and "Sex is not prescriptive or a progression" and "I can want sex more than him" and "I'm in charge of my sexual well being. I'm not putting that on my partner any longer." Now these are the echoes I'm starting to hear from the minority that are not only displeased with our past sexual legacy, but also are willing to do something about it. I'll call them the *shifters*. This new narrative is not yet embraced by the majority of our collective body, but it's a good start.

A little while ago, I was at a BYU football game with my second son. As is typical, the fans started a wave that went around the stadium a few times. In some ways, the needed shift in our cultural narrative is like a wave at a sports game. One person can start it but more than one needs to be involved in order for the wave to take form and round the stadium. It is a little nerve racking for some to start the wave. They think, "Will others follow if I stand up and lift my arms into the air, or will I look like a fool?" As one is followed by a few other brave fans, it becomes easier for the fans next to them to stand up and raise their arms into the air. Soon the wave has taken form and is on its hypnotizing way around the stadium. The first few brave fans of our new sexual narrative have stood up and raised their arms. Let us not leave them feeling foolish. Rather, let us all stand up and proudly raise our arms in the air and experience a shift in the way that the LDS population experiences, discusses, and treats sexuality.

Let us be a sex positive, affirming, supporting, enjoying, and loving people. We are in control of creating a sexual legacy for the generations to follow. Join the voices of those unhappy with our old cultural past narrative about sexuality and be instead sex positive. Let's create a sexual legacy that the generations to come will be proud of. Let us no longer be the sexually anorexic population that we've become known as. Rather, let's rise up as a conservative people that are known to enjoy sex and value its relevance in our marriage and in our individual lives. Who else is going to say to the world "Sex can feel good, bring us closer to our spouse, and connect us with God"? We can! In a world that values almost exclusively the physical aspects of sex, it is our responsibility to add to the world narrative that sex not only feels good and can make us feel more attached to our spouse, but it can also be and feel spiritual. Wouldn't that be a sexual legacy to be proud of?

There are already those first few people standing up raising their arms in the air to shift the LDS sexual narrative. Perhaps there are some ways that we can re-story some of our sexual past. I'm not talking about fabricating anything. Rather, emphasizing the sex-positive aspects of our LDS culture to help our new narrative along. For example, Utah is the state with the most births per capita. Sometimes it's easy to get pregnant but for many, pregnancy doesn't come very easily. That's a lot of sex the Utah Mormons are having! Married couples also typically have more sex than single people despite what media would have the world believe. LDS religion values marriage as much or more than any other group of people that I know. It is a logical thought progression then to think that LDS members have a great deal of sex. I challenge each of you that truly want to be the progenitors of a sex-positive LDS sexual culture to re-story our sexual past and continue to emphasize our new sexual narrative.

In his chapter entitled "The Fountain of Life" in the *Eternal Marriage Student Manual*,[1] President Boyd K. Packer discusses aspects of our creation, heritage, existence, journey, and destination that I think will be helpful as we re-story our cultural past and shift it to be sex positive, which will in turn lead to healthier sexuality for us as a people.

There are three parts of this chapter that stand out to me as profound and will help to re-story our LDS narrative about sexuality to be more positive. The first relates to his reference to scripture in Abraham. "The Gods went down to organize man in their own image, in the image of the Gods to form they him, male and female to form they them. And the Gods said: We will bless them. And the Gods said: We will cause them to be fruitful and multiply, and replenish the earth, and subdue it" (Abraham 4:27–28). One of the very first things that God wanted for this couple was to bless them by Adam and Eve having children. Our heritage begins with God blessing Adam and Eve to find joy in their sexual relationship.

The second part that stands out to me relates to the following quote. "The commandment to multiply and replenish the earth has never been rescinded. It is essential to the plan of redemption and is the source of human happiness. Through the righteous exercise of this power, as through nothing else, we may come close to our Father in Heaven and experience a fulness of joy, even godhood! The power of procreation is not an incidental part of the plan of happiness; it is the key—the very key."[2] That's pretty powerful. President Packer said that through exercising this relationship, and *nothing* else, we will find the fulness of joy and be close to godhood. It is the very key to the plan of happiness. So our sexual relationship is a vital part of God's plan for us.

Third, happiness, joy, and exaltation depend on how we respond to our sexuality. Packer says, "The desire to mate in humankind is constant and very strong. Our happiness in mortal life, our joy and exaltation, are dependent upon how we respond to these persistent, compelling physical desires."[3] It appears to me that our LDS culture is thick with positive messages about sexuality and that sexuality is more a part of our beliefs than most have realized. Even more evident to me is that Satan would want to destroy these positive views of sexuality since it is essential to God's great plan of happiness for us. I have to say that unfortunately Satan appears to be winning in extinguishing how our culture feels about our sexual heritage and the importance that God has place on the sexual relationship. To me this is all the more reason to re-story and change our LDS cultural narrative about sex.

In the space below, write down some new narratives for our collective sexual past:

Below write down sex-positive thoughts that will help to create a new sexual narrative for our culture:

I am often asked, "How can sex be spiritual or make us feel connected with God? God is not what I'm thinking about during sex nor would I ever want to think of Him during sex." To be honest, I struggled with knowing what it meant to have a sex life that's spiritual and how to bring God into your sex life. I wrestled with this idea many times over. Right around the time that I started graduate school, I began developing some more solid ideas about what this meant and how a couple might create such an experience. As I grew as a therapist and in my understanding of sex therapy, so too did my knowledge of what a spiritually deprived sexual relationship looks like and what a spiritually nurtured sexual relationship looks like. To illustrate the difference, I want to provide a few examples.

NATASHA & TOM: A CASE STUDY ABOUT EMOTION AND SPIRITUALITY

Earlier today a couple nearing divorce came to my office. Natasha and Tom—among other things—discussed their sex life. Both described feeling physical pleasure during sex, but were very displeased with feeling disconnected and were nowhere near feeling spiritual or closer to God during sex. In fact, they ashamedly described their sex life feeling somewhat like a porno. Natasha and Tom were at a loss for how to change this. The couple had very little emotional engagement in their overall relationship. They didn't connect or feel that the other person even enjoyed being around or talking to them. Somehow despite this, they had sex regularly.

147

They were both at their wits end for how to change the sexual tone of their relationship. This couple did very little to bring connection and God into their sex life, maybe out of fear or due to the lack of knowhow. Either way, they were focusing on the physical to the neglect of the emotional and spiritual. Strictly focusing on the physical can be a lot easier because it doesn't require true presence and vulnerability.

SAMANTHA & ERIC: A CASE STUDY ABOUT EMOTIONAL FOREPLAY

Samantha and Eric were nearing the end of treatment and had lately been describing their sex life as the best sex of all time. Samantha said that she had never felt so close to him and strangely more connected to God when she and Eric had sex. Not only did they feel closer but they also almost paradoxically expressed feeling more erotic. We explored what this was like for them. Eric said that sex was more than just touching her or having an orgasm. Sure, he really enjoyed those things, but it was more than that at times. The couple had been making time to be vulnerable and really be seen and heard by the other partner. This meant inside and outside of the bedroom. Among other things, Samantha talked about her issues with feeling sexual arousal at the end of a long day. Eric expressed himself more lovingly and supportively as he once did when they were first married. Samantha felt the emotional foreplay that Eric was engaged with. Eric saw Samantha valuing their sexual time together and saying that it mattered to her personally. One could say that the couple was having emotional sex on a regular basis.

Eric soon felt that Samantha was showing up for sex in a way that she never had before—and not just for him. Samantha felt like more than her body with Eric and cherished the time he spent softly kissing her, sensually touching her skin, and looking into her eyes. They also had hot steamy rough sex that also felt close and connecting. This was due to them both showing up for each other, emotionally for Eric and sexually for Samantha. Before that time, Samantha described Eric as almost disconnected when they were sexual. Eric described Samantha in a similar way saying, "She's there obviously, but it's more like her body is there and her person is absent."

After these new sexual encounters, the couple felt like they were on cloud nine—mostly because of their connection with one another.

Eric felt seen, valued, and heard. He also saw, respected, and listened to Samantha and vice versa. Lying in bed, quickly getting dressed to get breakfast for the kids, over text—it didn't matter. Samantha and Eric felt the divine in their relationship. They experienced what they thought was the way that God wanted them to enjoy each other. This only came in and through vulnerability and true intent to connect. They were no longer having sex as the world teaches. They learned to be their own teachers and listen to their internal needs that said different things to each of them. Then Samantha and Eric became daring and shared their vulnerability. Their spouse listened and was there for them, which only increased further vulnerability. The outcome was feeling God's presence in their relationship due to their sexual relationship.

Use the space below to write down some ways that you can show up and be seen by your partner. Also, write down what prevents you from intent to connect as well as follow through. Then work on eliminating these roadblocks and fostering more intent to connect. Vulnerability is not going to happen if your partner is truly unsafe. If this is not something that the two of you can change on your own then do not waste any time allowing things to get worse. Meet with a therapist to create a safe space in your marriage where vulnerability can present itself.

❧ NOTES ☙

1. Boyd K. Packer, "The Fountain of Life," in *Eternal Marriage Student Manual* (Church Educational System manual, 2003, 141–146).
2. Packer, 141.
3. Packer, 141.

"THE TALK"

*I*n her fascinating book on sexual education, *Not Under My Roof: Parents, Teens, and the Culture of Sex*,[1] Amy Schalet examines the differences in outcomes of and approach to sexual education of the United States and the Netherlands. Amy highlights many significant findings. She reports that the rates of teen pregnancy are one of the highest in the United States and one of the lowest in the Netherlands.[2] Comparing these two countries, she goes on to say that American teenagers are twice as likely to have abortions and eight times as likely to give birth as teenagers in the Netherlands.[3] American teenagers also account for more than one quarter of all STIs (sexually transmitted infections) in the United States.[4] Comparatively, the rates of HIV and STIs in the Netherlands are extremely low. Dutch teenagers are the top users of contraceptives at the time of first intercourse, and they have high rates of birth control use—the pill—when they are sexually active. Sixty-six percent of sexually active American teens regret having sex for the first time at the time they did. This is a stark contrast when most of the sexually active teenagers in the Netherlands say that sex was "wanted and fun" when speaking of their first time having sex.[5] Do teenagers in the Netherlands have an early age of first intercourse due to the early age of sexual education? The answer is no. Actually, their age of first intercourse is the same as that of the age of first intercourse for American teens on average.

So what accounts for these dramatically different outcomes? The difference is said to mostly be due to the differing approach to sexual education between the two countries. Before the sexual revolution, the focus of sexual education was on the negative elements of sex. The United States continued this old mindset and introduced abstinence-only programs into schools. In the Netherlands, their sexual education is much more comprehensive. They do not simply focus on disease control or intercourse, but on the large aspects of sexuality. Sexual assertiveness that aids in preventing sexual coercion and education on emotional intimacy are just some of the components they stress in their comprehensive approach. I believe that fear has driven closed lips about sexuality in our culture and the United States as a whole. It appears that the fear may be that talking about sex will be more like an instruction manual for our youth. As you can see, talking about sexuality in the Netherlands has had almost the opposite effect. As the we are seeing with the Netherlands, teenagers will likely abstain when they have options, knowledge, words, and alternatives. Women are generally more risk prone with sex when they are less educated. Knowledge therefore really is power. I believe it is the same for men. The point in me highlighting these differences is not political but to show that the approach that many of us have used needs to change. I have just touched on some of the fascinating elements of the Netherlands's approach to sexuality. I urge you to explore more.

Being one of the only sex therapists in Utah has afforded me the opportunity to hear plenty of shocking stories about "the talk" that many of my clients were given when they were younger. Just in case you are not following, "the talk" I'm referring to is the age-old discussion of sex that young girls and boys get from their parents. While I'm always relieved to hear that a talk about sex occurred, I can't say that I've ever been impressed by how the parents communicated about intimacy, sexuality, biology, and reproduction. While most instances where "the talk" occurred have been better than if no talk took place, I have had the misfortune of hearing about sex talks that were far more damaging than if nothing would have been said at all.

Just as I discussed the new LDS cultural narrative about sex, *shifting*, we need a new "talk" about sex for our children. We as LDS or conservative people are not the only ones that are lacking in the sex talk department. This is an epidemic even for liberal parents throughout the United States. Research has shown that parents are failing their children in this regard. I'm calling this shift in how we must discuss sex (intimacy, sexuality, biology, and reproduction) with our children "the new talk."

One of the differences with the new talk versus the old talk is that the new talk is ongoing and integrated into everyday life. The old talk happened once or maybe two or three times if you were lucky—perhaps unlucky depending on how well your parents communicated about difficult topics as well as their perspective on aspects of sex. A handful of instances where "the talk" occurred, at best, are not enough time for parents to communicate all of the important elements of intimacy, sexuality, biology, and reproduction. Not only do parents need more time to communicate these important topics, but children, teenagers, and young adults need time for the information to sink in so that follow up questions or remarks can be made. Additionally, our intimate, sexual, biological and reproductive development occurs across time and not at one static point, so new questions and musings will occur throughout time. Thus, dimensions of the sex talk need to be addressed as the child develops. The old talk doesn't allow for appropriate time needed, pondering and re-entering conversation, or discussion that evolves and changes along the child's developmental trajectory. I believe that part of the reason why parents don't have ongoing conversations and provide their children with the important information related to intimacy, sexuality, biology, and reproduction are because the parents don't really know themselves. Thus, a downward spiral in sex-positive views of sexuality and knowledge takes place. The concept of the blind leading the blind has never been as true as in this example.

I was asked by one of my colleagues when "the talk" should take place. I simply replied, "Right now." Parents need to have the talk right away and it continues on into adulthood! It doesn't matter the age of the child. Start at the next great opportunity or create the next opportunity. Parents of babies can describe and name the child's sexual anatomy as they would with any other body part. It's just as important for children to know their sexual anatomy as the rest of their body parts. What message is being communicated when a parent doesn't teach about the child's penis, vulva, and vagina? I believe this teaches the child that these body parts aren't important. Additionally, this tells the child that there is something strange about these body parts and that the parents might feel some shame for the penis, vulva, and vagina. In turn, the lesson is that the child might also need to feel shame for their unnamed body parts

153

and what these parts make them feel or what they do with said parts. Interestingly, when parents do name the sexual organs, most parents provide the name of their son's penis, but not their daughter's vulva or vagina. This then plays out in later life as the teenager rarely does graffiti of the vulva. You are more likely to see images of the penis. It's no wonder that many women grow up differentiated from their sexuality and anatomy. How is a woman that grew up separated from her vulva supposed to teach her spouse or know herself what she needs with regard to sex?

When children ask their parents where babies come from or how and why they were in their mother's tummy, the parents can age appropriately discuss aspects of reproduction. Answer your child's questions. If they are asking then that is one sign that they are ready to know at some level. At the same time, don't just wait for your child to ask you. Some children are more curious about such topics than others. Find moments to slip into conversations and education about bodies and reproduction.

When your child is exploring their vulva or penis and you walk in on them or see them touching themselves as you are giving them a bath, let them know that such touch does feel good and is a very beautiful part of who they are. Do not shame them or make them feel like there is something wrong with them. Usually, the child will stop on their own once there has been a little education about why this feels good and when they realize that what they feel and want to do is normal.

Begin having conversations about love and various components of intimacy long before your child falls in love. Talk about the love between you and your spouse. After a long kiss with your spouse, you can express how much you care about your partner and that kissing them or talking to them are some ways that you enjoy sharing that intimacy. This will help your child learn that emotional and sexual expression within a relationship are healthy and normal. The Spirit will talk to their soul and express through warmth and inspiration that what you are saying is true. I've seen my children smile and giggle as I kiss my wife and say such things to them after an expression of love. I know that the Spirit is confirming this truth to them.

These are but a few examples of how one can slip into "the new talk" about intimacy, sexuality, biology, and reproduction with their children. It is by no means an exhaustive list. I'd like for you to think of this as the early beginnings of a longer list that I'd like for you to create below. Write down some ways that you can slip into the new talk with your children or teenagers or young adults and perhaps adult children. If you start thinking of ways that you can have the new talk with your teenager or young adult and she or he is only three at the time, then you are beginning to shift into the new talk mentality. Not only will you be more prepared for those future discussions, but you will also have a new shift in how you think about "the talk" as one that is ongoing.

The old talk was formal, well prepared—almost scripted—out of the norm, and reeked of discomfort. While it is admiral of those parents that have had the old talk with their children, what all of this creates is an environment that is anything but conducive of ongoing conversation, and it communicates the wrong message to the child. The old talk is communicating that if future conversations are to occur that they must be under similar conditions of formality, otherwise it will be strange and borderline inappropriate. The old talk is unconsciously saying that this is so out of the norm that we must go to a special place, use soft voices, sit in a dark corner or the ice cream parlor, isolate from your siblings, and so on in order to discuss your body, sex, or these new feelings you are having. Even if an invitation to answer any future questions is provided, the child is going to feel so awkward that they will rarely, if ever, accept such an invitation.

The dual message that comes from the context and verbalization are conflictual and misleading to children. The parent is saying that the changes they are experiencing or going to experience are normal and good, but the drama given to the topic is sending a far different message. One that communicates to the child that intimacy, sexuality, biology, and reproduction are awkward, obscure, secretive, and something unrelated to everyday life etc. As I have seen as a sex therapist, perhaps one of the most damaging unintentional messages related to sexual self schemas is that the parents are unwittingly communicating that intimacy, sexuality, biology, and reproduction are not a congruent part of one's person to be intermixed with life and experienced within the parameters of normal everyday life. Instead they are unconsciously communicating that one must conjure up or access these elements of the person within special situations more like an event. These messages internalized make it difficult for one to experience life as a sexualized person. Rather the person has to make exceptions and go out of their way to access their sexuality. I have seen firsthand how difficult it is for someone to go out of their way to access their sexuality when they did not learn how to go about everyday life as a sexualized person, the way that they were intended to be.

We as members of the LDS church have a stronger need to be open with our children and send correct ongoing messages for a number of reasons. First, the LDS population is at the onset of a new cultural narrative surrounding sex. More voices are being sex positive and promoting. It's truly an amazing time to be LDS. To fully bring about this movement and cultural paradigm shift, the culture needs our voices and the voices of our children to overhaul how our culture thinks, feels, and communicates about sex.

Second, we have a clear picture about our godly nature and heritage. A crucial part of that lies in us getting bodies and having experiences in our bodies. We know that we are created in the image of God and by God. It appears as though Heavenly Father has a plan for us that includes fundamentally having and using all of our God-given body parts. It is likely to assume then that God wants us to use our bodies within our marriage as a means of pleasure, connection, joy, and fulfillment. He wants us to feel the joy that is inherently programmed into our biological makeup; to function and feel as He himself designed. We are created to feel immense sexual pleasure as designed by God. Not only did God create our bodies to feel these amazing things upon this earth, but we also know that our spirits will have similar properties. It is logical to assume then that our spirits will have similar though escalated experiences with our eternal companion in the celestial kingdom. Lastly, sexual expression foundationally bonds and attaches us to our spouse. We literally imprint all aspects of our relationship and person onto another. Sexual expression is a magnificent way to imprint joy, connection, pleasure, and relational bliss onto our partner.

Third, who better to teach our children than their parents? Your kids will be taught about bodies and sexuality from someone. Like never before, the Internet has been serving as a form of sexual education. In this technological era, it is undoubtedly going to occur. We have seen historically that no information or limited information gives rise to some pretty serious sexual issues, but I don't think many of us are aware or prepared for what is to come if we leave the educating up to peers and whatever our kids find online. However, that is exactly what is taking place inside and out of the Church. Knowing that a lot of education about intimacy, sexuality, biology, and reproduction is going to occur as your child grows and develops, don't you want to be the voice of truth that your child can hear through the fog of inaccuracy and misconception? We as parents need to be informed and then have the new talk regularly so that the Spirit can witness to them the truthfulness of our teachings.

Fourth, your child's intimacy, sex, body, and reproduction-positive self-schema will act as a life preserver. We all know how complex the world is and is mounting to become. It is increasingly more difficult to hold fast to values and our religion. Acceptance has inadvertently bred indifference and amoral beliefs that pull at the sacred marriage. Through the development of sexual self-schemas that are sex positive, our children will have a life preserver to buoy them up.

The old mentality was to limit the information that was given to children about sex because it might cause them to become curious and to act on what was told or taught to them. Along with the new talk comes a shift in mentality that tells us that the more our children know about appropriate intimacy, sexuality, biology, and reproduction, the better safeguarded and protected they are. Obviously, this information needs to be age appropriate and accurate.

REY: A CASE STUDY ABOUT SEXUAL EDUCATION

Rey had grown up in a conservative home where there was limited information about sex. She had kind of had the old "talk" with her mom one day after school on the ride home. Rey felt uncomfortable and was successful at derailing the "talk" after a few attempts at changing the conversation. Her mother had taught her about menses and the changes in her breast size, but that was about it.

By the age of fourteen, Rey had heard sexual terms in multiple arenas of her life. She had regrettably made out several times with some boys her friends introduced her to. She had been groped by two boys during school without realizing what took place at the time. She had been pressured to let a guy she liked touch her breasts on one occasion because he told her that "she can't just turn a guy on and leave him that way." He told her that it "wasn't good for his body." She had also looked up sexual material online over the years because she was curious about some of the things her friends were doing with boys and the changes she was experiencing. Through her searches, she found various types of pornography that were both arousing and disturbing. She tried out masturbation but didn't really know what she was trying to accomplish. Rey had also started to dress more revealing because she found that was a helpful way of getting the attention she sought from a few boys in her neighborhood. Throughout these sexual experiences, Rey also nurtured the friendship of Patrick, a boy from a neighboring ward, and had a really good first kiss when she was twelve.

Rey's parents, while well meaning, could have helped to create a "life preserver" both in her lived sexual experiences and in her future romantic relationships. If her parents would have had ongoing conversations over her lifespan about intimacy, sexuality, biology, and reproduction, Rey might have had different sexual experiences. She may have not felt the urge to go online and look up sexual acts and other explicit material. Perhaps she and her parents could look up some more accurate and non-pornographic imagery and information together. She would have had the relationship with her parents where she could talk to them about her body exploration, thoughts, feelings, and behaviors she was engaging in. Rey may have been more aware of what was going on when she was groped and not felt as responsible and ashamed as she did once she realized she had been taken advantage of. Rey could have had a healthy view of romantic intimacy and felt positive impressions more easily when she engaged in healthy interactions, such as her friendship with Patrick. She would have identified unhealthy intimacy in herself and her friends, such as making out with boys she had no emotional connection with and seeking attention through sexually reveling clothing.

With the mentality of the new talk, parents like Rey's could provide a life preserver that a child could use well into adulthood. Rey's awareness and encouraged experiences of healthy intimacy could keep her safe in an often-confusing world that teaches inaccurate messages about how to find, build, and nurture relationships. Her parents could have equipped her with a life preserver that she could use when she finds herself in or near troubling waters that otherwise may engulf her. In this way, she can more astutely navigate the intimate relational world.

Rey's sexuality could have been embarked upon with excitement and enthusiasm should the new talk been her parents' strategy. An adult Rey would have a very clear idea of who she is sexually and be proud to express this sexuality appropriately within relationships and eventually with her spouse. She'd be an equal sexual match for any prepared partner. She would have a clear knowledge of how sexuality fits into her divine godly heritage. She'd know that a critical part of God's plan was for her to have a body and to have experiences while in her body. Rey's parents could have communicated that as being created in God's image, we possess sexual feelings and potential that He not only wants and expects for us, but that he too possesses and feels. Rey would have a clear understanding of what sexual changes would take place, and why, and feel proud to be a sexual being as part of her godly heritage. The adult Rey would be able to think back with fondness to her sexual development. In this way Rey would be able to use the life preserver her parents helped provide her with by honoring that heritage and using her robustly nourished sexuality within her marriage to keep it alive and flourishing.

Rey's biological understanding would act in a similar fashion in her adult relationships to keep her afloat within her marriage. She would have a deep understanding of how sexual expression foundationally bonds and attaches us to those we sexually relate to and would relish in this with her eternal companion. She'd have a healthy relationship with her vulva, vagina, and breasts. This relationship and respect for her sexual biology would include being kind and loving toward her body and passion for its capacity—such a relationship that would elevate her marital intimacy. Sexual expression with her spouse could feel entirely vulnerable and be a way of honoring her body.

Rey's understanding of the reproductive nature of men and women could also act as a life preserver throughout her life by helping her to see that she is more than a uterus and potential temporary home to future babies. Many women in our culture get aspects of "the talk" that only teach about the reproductive role of female anatomy. This communicates a strong message to women that their sexual anatomy is basically for creating children. While it is imperative that both men and women understand about reproduction and their specific roles therein, women especially need to hear that their sexual anatomy is for more than reproduction. In respecting these two roles, Rey would be able to grow into a woman that cherishes her divine privilege as a potential mother while also nurturing her sexual self-schema that she is a sexual being.

Fifth, the new talk will aid in the new LDS cultural narrative about sex and contribute to the cultural shift in which has barely already begun. Your children will grow up with the strong identification within the Church that they were part of the new generation that was sex positive. They will be the beneficiaries of healthy sex lives in which their marriages will be strengthened because of.

In sum, start having the new talk today. Don't dodge questions. Stay age appropriate. Find natural moments to infuse their understanding with sex and body-positive messages that link back to our godly heritage. Formal discussions communicate messages that might make it hard for children to open up since a big deal was made about this topic. The new talk is ongoing not a once or twice occurrence. It may be weekly, monthly, or vary from kid to kid and time period.

❧ Notes ❧

1. Amy Schalet, *Not Under My Roof: Parents, Teens, and the Culture of Sex* (Chicago: The University of Chicago Press, 2011).
2. Amy Schalet, "The Sleepover Question," *New York Times*, July 23, 2011, http://www.nytimes.com/2011/07/24/opinion/sunday/24schalet.html/.
3. Carrie Weisman, "Attitudes and Outcomes of Sex Ed: The US vs. the Netherlands," *Truth-Out.org*, March 29, 2015, http://www.truth-out.org/news/item/29920-attitudes-and-outcomes-of-sex-ed-the-us-vs-the-netherlands/.
4. Weisman.
5. Saskia de Melker, "The Case for Starting Sex Education in Kindergarten," *PBS.org*, May 27, 2015, http://www.pbs.org/newshour/updates/spring-fever/.

CONCLUSION

T here may have been many of you who read through this book and applied principles, activities, and concepts but still struggle in your sexual relationship. Perhaps your specific issues were not touched on or elaborated on enough for the severity of your problem. I want to offer this conclusion as a way for you to know what you are looking for by way of a therapist. Finding the right professional to help you through this aspect of your relationship is just as important as finding a medical doctor who can help you with a specific illness or medical diagnosis.

The research states that the therapeutic alliance, or the relationship that you have with your therapist, is the most influential factor in you getting the help you seek out of therapy. So to begin, look for someone you can trust, you feel safe with, or you connect with. Give therapy a few sessions to feel this out, or talk with the therapist on the phone to get an idea. Next, most therapists have had a class on sex therapy, gone to a conference, or had a handful of clients who have sexual issues. This in no way makes them specialists in sex therapy. They may, however, state this on their websites or professional bios. Investigate what it is that makes them specialists. Do not be afraid to ask them on the phone and to hold off on scheduling an appointment while you look around for other therapists. Additionally, sex therapy includes psychological education and between-session activities (homework). If you are not being assigned activities and working on your sexual relationship outside of therapy, you most likely won't get the changes you desire. Lastly, if you think you are meeting with a therapist to work on your sexual issues and the therapist spends most of the time talking about your relationship and often glosses over your sexual relationship, you are probably meeting with a therapist who doesn't know how to work with sexual issues.

WORKS CITED

Amen, Daniel G. *Sex on the Brain: 12 Lessons to Enhance Your Love Life.* New York: Three Rivers Press, 2008.

Basson, Rosemary. "The Female Sexual Response: A Different Model," Journal of Sex & Marital Therapy, 2000.

Busby, Dean M., Jason S. Carrol, and Chelom Leavitt. *Sexual Wholeness in Marriage: An LDS Perspective on Integrating Sexuality and Spirituality in Our Marriages.* United States of America: Book Printers of Utah, 2013.

Carnes, Patrick. "Sexual Addiction and Compulsion: Recognition, Treatment, and Recovery." *CNS Spectrums* 5, no. 10 (2000): 63–72.

de Melker, Saskia. "The Case for Starting Sex Education in Kindergarten." *PBS.org.* May 27, 2015. http://www.pbs.org/newshour/updates/spring-fever/.

Eichel, Edward and Nobile, Philip. (1992) "The Perfect Fit: How to Achieve Mutual Fulfillment and Monogamous Passion Through the New Intercourse" Dutton Books.

Haltia, Lauri T., Antti Viljanen, Riitta Parkkola, Nina Kemppainen, Juha O. Rinne, Pirjo Nuutila, and Valtteri Kaasinen. "Brain White Matter Expansion in Human Obesity and the Recovering Effect of Dieting." *Journal of Clinical Endocrinology & Metabolism* 92, no. 8 (2007): 3278–84. https://doi.org/10.1210/jc.2006-2495.

Hilton, Donald L., Jr. *He Restoreth My Soul: Understanding and Breaking the Chemical and Spiritual Chains of Pornography Addiction through the Atonement of Jesus Christ.* San Antonio, Texas: Forward Press Publishing, 2009.

Holland, Jeffrey R. "Of Souls, Symbols, and Sacraments." Brigham Young University devotional. Provo, UT. 1988. http://emp.byui.edu/WARDD/honors221/articles/souls.htm.

———. "Personal Purity." *Ensign.* November 1998.

"Is There Such a Thing as 'Soul Mates'?" *New Era.* Nov. 2013.

Johnson, Sue. "Attachment and the Dance of Sex: Integrating Couple and Sex Therapy." DrSueJohnson.com. Accessed Oct. 24, 2017. http://www.drsuejohnson.com/attachment-sex/attachment-and-the-dance-of-sex-integrating-couple-and-sex-therapy/.

———. "Shaping Love: A Seminal Study." DrSueJohnson.com. Accessed Oct. 24, 2017. http://drsuejohnson.com/science-2/shaping-love-a-seminal-study/.

Ju Kim, Seog, In Kyoon Lyoo, Jaeuk Hwang, Ain Chung, Hoon Sung Young, Jihyun Kim, Do Hoon Kwon, Hyun Chang Kee, and Perry F. Renshaw. "Prefrontal Grey-Matter Changes in Short-Term and Long-Term Abstinent Methamphetamine Abusers." *International Journal of Neuropsychopharmocology* no. 9 (2006): 221–228. doi:10.1017/S1461145705005699.

Kaplan, Helen S., PE: *How to Overcome Premature Ejaculation*, Brunner Mazel/New York Times, 1989.

Kaplan, Helen S., and Melvin Horwith. *The Evaluation of Sexual Disorders: Psychological and Medical Aspects*. New York: Brunner/Mazel, 1983. Print.

Kaplan, Helen S., "The New Sex Therapy: Active Treatment of Sexual Dysfunctions." Oxford, England: Brunner/Mazel, 1974.

Kimball, Spencer W. In Edward Kimbal, ed., *The Teachings of Spencer W. Kimball*. Salt Lake City: Deseret Book, 1982.

Masters, William H. and Johnson, Virginia E., *Human Sexual Inadequacy*. Boston: Little, Brown, 1970.

Masters, William H., and Johnson, Virginia E., *Human Sexual Response*, Bantam, 1981 ISBN 978-0-553-20429-2; 1st ed. 1966.

McCarthy, Barry W., and Michael E. Metz. *Men's Sexual Health: Fitness for Satisfying Sex*. New York: Taylor & Francis, 2008.

Metz, Michael E., and Barry W. McCarthy. "The 'Good-Enough Sex' Model for Couple Sexual Satisfaction." *Sexual and Relationship Therapy* 22, no. 3 (2007): 351–62. http://dx.doi.org/10.1080/14681990601013492/.

Packer, Boyd K. "The Fountain of Life." In *Eternal Marriage Student Manual*. Church Educational System manual, 2003, 141–146.

Perel, Esther. "The Secret to Desire in a Long-Term Relationship." Filmed February 2013 in New York, NY. TED video. 19:03. https://www.ted.com/talks/esther_perel_the_secret_to_desire_in_a_long_term_relationship/.

Prescott, Marianne Holman. "How to Teach Children about Sexual Intimacy." *Church News*. March 16, 2015. https://www.lds.org/church/news/how-to-teach-children-about-sexual-intimacy/.

Schalet, Amy. *Not Under My Roof: Parents, Teens, and the Culture of Sex*. Chicago: The University of Chicago Press, 2011.

———. "The Sleepover Question." *New York Times*. July 23, 2011. http://www.nytimes.com/2011/07/24/opinion/sunday/24schalet.html/.

Schnarch, David. *Passionate Marriage: Love, Sex, and Intimacy in Emotionally Committed Relationships*. New York: W. W. Norton, 1997.

Simon, William, and John H. Ganon. "Sexual Scripts: Permanence and Change." *Archives of Sexual Behavior* 15, no. 2 (April 1986): 97–120. http://doi.org/10.1007/BF01542219.

Sternberg, Robert J. "A Triangular Theory of Love." *Psychological Review* 93, no. 2 (1986): 119–35.

The Church of Jesus Christ of Latter-day Saints. "Family Home Evening: Sexual Intimacy Is Sacred and Beautiful." Overcoming Pornography. September 1, 2016. https://www.overcomingpornography.org/spouses-and-families/sexual-intimacy-is-sacred-and-beautiful?lang=eng.

Vernacchio, Al. "Sex Needs a New Metaphor. Here's one . . ." Filmed March 2012 in New York, NY. TED video. 8:18. https://www.ted.com/talks/al_vernacchio_sex_needs_a_new_metaphor_here_s_one/.

Weeks, Gerald R., Nancy Gambescia, and Katherine M. Hertlein. *A Clinician's Guide to Systemic Sex Therapy*. 2nd ed. New York: Taylor & Francis, 2016.

Weisman, Carrie. "Attitudes and Outcomes of Sex Ed: The US vs. the Netherlands." *Truth-Out.org*. March 29, 2015. http://www.truth-out.org/news/item/29920-attitudes-and-outcomes-of-sex-ed-the-us-vs-the-netherlands/.

ABOUT the AUTHOR

D r. Anthony A. Hughes holds a PhD in marriage and family therapy from Brigham Young University (BYU). He is a licensed marriage and family therapist in the state of Utah and an AAMFT approved supervisor. Dr. Hughes is also a Certified Sex Therapist. He is the owner of Covenant Sex Therapy, located in Provo, Pleasant Grove, and Sandy, Utah, and is actively involved in clinical work there. He mentors several therapists working at his various clinics. Dr. Hughes is an adjunct graduate faculty member at Brigham Young University and Argosy University in their Marriage and Family Therapy departments and teaches courses about sex therapy and practicum. He also teaches sex therapy for Brigham Young University's graduate Social Work program. He has supervised many therapists providing therapy to clientele who deal with sexual issues. He has also been published in a peer-reviewed journal. Dr. Hughes has guest lectured on various occasions at Brigham Young University and Utah Valley University. He has similarly presented at Brigham Young University and Argosy, where continuing education units have been offered for his lectures on sexuality.

He has lectured for family medicine residents as well. Additionally, He has presented at national and state venues on the topic of sexuality. Dr. Hughes has also developed a revolutionary app, available at the Apple app store, to help couples improve their sexual relationship called *Sexual Healing*.

Dr. Hughes is very involved in his family life and thinks of his family time as the highlight of his life. His wife is also a therapist, which adds to the fulfillment that he finds in his marriage. Besides his wife, his children are the light of his life. Dr. Hughes currently lives in Pleasant Grove, Utah, and enjoys doing anything active, such as basketball, snow-boarding, wakeboarding, water-skiing, running, and yard work—yes, yard work.

Scan to visit

covenantsextherapy.com